Storytelling
At Its Best

Frank Ball

Storytelling at Its Best
A Practical Guide for Telling Stories

By Frank Ball

First Printing

 Roaring Lambs Publishing
17110 Dallas Pkwy Ste 260
Dallas, TX 75248

Phone: 972.380.0123

Email: info@RoaringLambs.org
        FBall@RoaringLambs.org

RoaringLambs.org

FrankBall.org

*With all the rules
we need to know,
what pleases the reader
matters most.*

Table of Contents

Going Deeper _____ 1

The Best Point of View _____ 6

The Best Sense of Time _____ 14

Finding the Best Story _____ 24

Seven Essential Storytelling Blocks _____ 30

    Situation _____ 34

    Character _____ 39

    Objective _____ 48

    Obstacles _____ 52

    Plight _____ 57

    Insight & Transformation _____ 61

    Unresolved Problem _____ 64

    Putting SCOOP into Practice _____ 66

The Writing Process _____ 69

Poetry _____ 75

Building Great Sentences _____ 80

Sharp Detail and Vivid Color _____ 85

Dealing with Dialog _____ 97

Punctuation _____ 102

    Apostrophe _____ 103

    Colon _____ 106

    Comma _____ 108

    Dash _____ 112

    Ellipsis _____ 114

Exclamation Mark_____ 116

Hyphen_____ 117

Parentheses_____ 119

Period_____ 121

Question Mark _____ 123

Quotation Marks_____ 126

Semicolon_____ 127

Slash _____ 129

Parts of Speech _____ 131

Adjectives _____ 133

Adverbs _____ 136

Conjunctions _____ 140

Interjections _____ 143

Nouns_____ 144

Prepositions _____ 146

Pronouns _____ 149

Verbs _____ 154

Capitalization _____ 157

Spelling_____ 162

Story Killers _____ 165

Practice Writing _____ 174

Getting Published _____ 178

Appendix _____ 187

Christianese _____ 189

Citing Sources_____ 193

Quoting Scripture _____ 195

Contranyms _____ 198

Expressions, Posture, and Actions _____ 201

Prepositional Verbs_____ 207

Redundant Words_____ 210

Shades of Meaning _____ 215

Throwaway Words _____ 227

Writing Prompts_____ 229

Scriptures for Storytellers _____ 232

Recommended Resources_____ 241

About the Author_____ 242

Going Deeper

Writers who trust the Lord will find strength in him. They'll be like eagles with spread wings, soaring on the wind. They'll be like the runner who has the stamina to finish the race or the hiker who won't faint when the climbing gets tough. — Isaiah 40:31

Never in history has the storytelling perspective been more important than now. No longer can we simply *tell* what happened. That's just boring news.

Remember the good old days.

A shrinking number of today's readers can remember life before television—when the family sat around the radio and listened to stories. That was the first evolutional step from reading books.

Sitting around the radio set, listeners heard the door slam. They heard people shouting. The sound of thunder shook them in their seats as pictures formed in their minds. They only *heard* the loud boom. For the picture, they had to imagine streaks of lightning flashing across the sky and feel like they were getting soaked from the rain.

They had no idea what life would be like with moving pictures on a screen—in color.

> Books today need to be as rewarding as watching a great movie.

Our modern world is different.

Today, movies provide setting, sound, and action. Music sets the mood of calm or panic, mystery or suspense, tragedy or comedy. Action, expressions, and dialog show the emotion. Virtually

1

nothing is left to our imaginations. We don't need a message across the bottom of the screen to tell us when someone is angry. We see it. We feel it. We are changed by it, because we are there. In the intensity of the moment, we forget that we're sitting on the couch, watching a Netflix movie.

If you want your readers to have a boring story that will put them to sleep, tell what happened. If you want to keep them awake, holding their interest, you must *show*, not *tell*. A life story can either be shown in a two-hour movie or be told in a book that could take two weeks to read. Which is better?

Books *can* be better, but without a deep point of view that delivers an experience more real than a movie, most people won't invest weeks when only a few hours will let them experience all they wanted.

Time is money.

Do the math. Suppose a two-hour movie is worth the viewer's time at fifteen dollars per hour, or $30 total. A 100,000-word novel takes the average reader about seven hours, or $105 total. As a writer, you are competing for the value of your audience's time. For your book to be worth three times the value of a movie, it must deliver an experience that is at least three times better.

Is this possible?

Yes.

> Writers must earn readers' time, not their money.

Nothing is more real to readers than the pictures, thoughts, and feelings from their own experiences. The fear and panic, thrills of victory, and depression from a heart-rending loss are most *real* in their imaginations when it's from their *personal* experiences. The vivid pictures, familiar sounds, and deep feelings come from what they've seen, heard, and felt before—with their own eyes and ears.

Since movies supply all the details, the viewers' imaginations aren't affecting them as much as what books have the power to do. While they're watching the screen, their engagement easily fades, and they drift off to sleep.

A huge difference exists between reading *about* a car crash, *seeing* a car crash, and *being in* the car crash. Movies let us see the car crash, which is better than reading about it. But a book with a deep point of view puts readers into the character in the car to experience the crash.

Nothing can be more engaging, so that's your goal. Make your writing so captivating that readers will say, "No movie is as good as this book."

Striving for excellence is easy.

Wanting your book to be better than a movie is a wonderful goal. Getting there is the tough part.

After writers visualize all that will happen in a scene, *telling* comes easy. Like sports reporters who saw the game, they can describe the field and what every player did. At the beginning, they can reveal who the heroes are and who will fail miserably. With this divine knowledge, they can reveal the final score at any point in the story.

Years ago, classical writing used this *telling* approach, and that was great back then. But today, great suspense and drama won't allow you to do those things. All but the most dedicated readers will be bored.

The difference between *showing* and *telling* is the place where readers put themselves in the scene. Are they standing with the narrator or reporter, seeing what's happening? That's *telling*. Or are they one character in the scene, who is sensing, interpreting, anticipating, and being affected by everything? That's *showing*.

> **Classical writing is no longer considered classy.**

Become the main character.

As you write, *being* the character instead of *describing* the character can be challenging. Why? Knowing what will happen next naturally begs you to be a reporter or observer. That's where outlining and character charts can be your worst enemy. When you have planned what will happen next, you risk overlooking the crucial details that would make readers stay awake, worrying, while including details that make good sleeping pills.

To solve this problem, put yourself into the mind of the character—who can only guess what will happen next. If you know, write as if you don't. Then push yourself even more passionately into that character's world until your descriptions focus on the joys and worries of that moment.

Not knowing brings worry and tension. Conditions may get better or worse, but they cannot remain the same for long, or boredom sets in. Fears may prove to be unfounded only to be followed by something that turns out to be even worse. Apparent failure leads to unexpected success. Dreams of glory wind up being nightmares. Repeatedly force yourself into the scene's main character and write as if nothing can be sensed beyond her thoughts and perceptions at that moment. The tension and suspense become true-to-life because you can only guess what might happen next. Your readers will be engaged because they must interpret what they are seeing in the story, anticipate the reactions, and be wrong most of the time.

> In *real* stories, readers visualize themselves as the main character.

Isn't that the way we walk through life every day? Yes, but at the end of the day, we easily forget our worries that didn't happen. To write about the day, we must remember what we thought could go wrong.

When a screenplay is written, people are chosen to play the parts. To do well with their role, they may need to lose or gain weight, acquire a different accent, or exhibit an entirely different appearance and personality from who they are in everyday life. They must do more than study the scene and learn their lines. As they *become* the character, they discover that some of the memorized lines and behaviors won't work for a true-to-life, believable scene.

Believability is crucial, both on the screen and on the page.

For a screenplay to be captivating, the plot lines and characterizations require adjustments as they are rehearsed and then made real in live-action.

The best way to have a multimillion-dollar movie fail at the box office is to have actors who aren't real in the way they play the part. At the first sign of forced

> The strength of fiction is its true-to-life believability.

expressions, faked tone of voice, or actions that don't quite fit the scene, believability is lost and viewers become disengaged. If that's true for movies, it's also true for our storytelling, because readers have developed a cinematic mindset. We must create scenes that contain the emotional thrills and chills, mystery and suspense, and the failures and successes that people experience all the time.

Life has only the present moment.

A story's characters should not remember the past without good reason. They anticipate the future without knowing what it will be, apprehensive that their worst fear could happen or confident that nothing will go wrong. But something will go right or wrong in a way they didn't expect. This "not knowing" creates tension that won't let readers sleep, because they are smart. They've seen enough to know that what looks so good can turn out terribly bad. And what they think are tragedies can lead to the greatest rewards.

That's what they expect, and we dare not disappoint them.

The Best Point of View

When I ponder what to write about, I remember the plights of my past and why I now give you praise. Then I reveal your glory by showing how you've worked in my life. — Psalm 143:5

Since you want readers *in* the action, not *observing* the action, your best narration comes from your point-of-view character in the scene. Movie producers use camera angles to focus on what's important and exclude what's not. We must use a limited focus with our descriptions to accomplish the same thing.

Don't give details that are unimportant to the character at that moment, are obvious from the context, or will be reasonably assumed.

Readers always assume the position of the narrator.

Where are you? Why are you there? What interests you at this moment? Out of all the things you as the point-of-view character *could* see, what *do* you see? Only what is most important to you at that moment. You pay virtually no attention to anything familiar—what you already know. If you as the author think some of those unimportant details are crucial for the reader, something needs to happen to make them important to your character.

Driving to work, what do you see along the way? You don't notice the things you see all the time. You might notice something new—eventually. Maybe on the fourth trip to work, you notice it for the first time. Why so long? It wasn't that important.

You've seen trains before. What's the big deal about this one? It's blocking the road and moving too slow. You're going to be late to work. You can't help but notice. Count the cars. Over a hundred. That's important to know when you have to face the boss. Now we have a familiar train that's worth mentioning, but be careful. Readers only want the details that are important to the character at that moment. Don't write about the

> If the narrator is an observer, readers watch the action from far away.

graffiti on the cars without showing how the character is affected. Why would you notice the difference between boxcars, flatbeds, oil tankers, and overseas containers? If it's not important to the character, it's not important to the story. Leave it out.

People notice something familiar when it either impedes or helps your progress. Something must be different about this drive, or there's no reason to notice. A car cuts in front of you and you swerve to avoid a wreck. Now that's a personal offense. The idiot! Where did he learn to drive? Obviously at offensive driving school. Those are the kinds of details readers want to know about.

The mission determines the message and how it needs to be told.

If the narrative doesn't touch the point-of-view character's emotions, it won't have much effect on readers. You have three grammatical perspectives through which your character's perceptions may be described.

Each one has its advantages for what it is and disadvantages for what it isn't. You can only choose one for each point-of-view character, so choose wisely.

Describe a simple *telling* scene.

Peter is minding his business after a frustrating night fishing. He and his partners have just finished stretching the 200' long by 15' high rectangular net on the shore to dry in the sun. It would rot if it were rolled up wet. Jesus walks up and asks if he caught anything, which is not a

7

*smart thing to ask a professional fisherman who hasn't caught anything.
Jesus tells him to drop the net from the other side of the boat, which is
stupid advice coming from a non-fisherman, but out of respect for Jesus,
Peter does it anyway. The subsequent unbelievably great catch of fish
makes Peter sorry that he ever doubted Jesus.*

Who is your point-of-view character in this scene? The narrator is
telling the story, so readers become an observer, watching what
Peter and Jesus do.

Now we want readers to see what happens as a character in the
scene. Who will that person be? Let's not be too quick with
choosing Peter. Who else was there? How might they have been
affected by what they saw?

Let's see, there are John, James, and Andrew. Zebedee could
have been there, somewhat upset that his sons kept chasing after
this Messiah instead of tending to their
work. How was the skeptical Pharisee
affected? How about someone who had
been listening to Jesus' message and
believed? Cornelius could have been there,
gathering information to report to Pilate. Or perhaps a blind man
was there, wanting to be healed. The possibilities are endless, and
each perspective can give readers a different, unexpected insight
about what happened.

> **Change in the character gives the scene value.**

No matter which point of view you choose, one thing is
crucial: your character must change by the end of the scene.
Without that change being evident, readers remain unchanged
and the scene has no significant value, no need to exist.

First Person: the point-of-view character is telling the story.

From Peter's point of view:

*After stretching the net on the shore to dry beneath the rising sun, I sat to
catch my breath and stared at the ground, tired after a frustrating night.
In my countless times on the lake, I never failed to catch plenty of fish,
but this time all I had for the market was rocks and sticks.*

"Did you catch anything?" Jesus was half-serious, half-smiling, as if he already knew the answer. "You should drop the net on the other side of the boat."

This is a simple introduction to what should take several pages to show how the event changed Peter's life. His story uses the first-person *I* perspective, limited to his perceptions at the moment.

Notice that Peter does not name himself or describe himself. He has no need to talk about his partners or what the weather is like. An observer would describe those things, but Peter wouldn't. If he wants to sit and sulk over catching no fish, that's all he would mention, and that's all readers should know at this point.

> **Readers see themselves as the first-person "I" in the story.**

A blind man's point of view:

Were the rumors about Jesus true? Hope drove me through the crowd, but then his voice moved away, toward the shouts in the distance. The tone of frustrated men lacked the usual pleasure of a fisherman's work overnight.

I pushed my walking stick forward, feeling my way to move closer. The sudden quiet of the men said Jesus must have walked up to them.

"Did you catch anything?" Jesus sounded like a rabbi, about to teach what his students didn't understand. "You should drop the net on the other side of the boat."

Notice that the blind man never says he is blind. He already knows that, so in a deep point of view, he's not allowed to give that information. Readers are left to discover that fact on their own, and they will. Again we're using the first-person *I* perspective in telling the story.

The words *I* and *me* only appear once in three paragraphs. We need no more than that in a deep point of view, because we're *showing* what the blind man saw. We're not telling that he saw it.

The blind man telling instead of showing:

I wondered if the rumors about Jesus were true. I had to find out, so I pushed my way through the crowd. I heard his voice move away, toward the shouts in the distance. I heard the tone of frustrated men. They lacked the usual pleasure of a fisherman's work overnight.

I pushed my walking stick forward, and I felt my way to move closer. I noticed the sudden quiet of the men, and I knew that Jesus must have walked up to them.

"Did you catch anything?" I thought Jesus sounded like a rabbi, about to teach what his students didn't understand. "You should drop the net on the other side of the boat."

This example is really bad to make clear an important point: a deep point of view must reveal the character's perceptions without *telling* clauses such as *I wondered, I felt, I heard, I thought,* and *I knew.*

Second Person: the reader is told what to think and do.

From Peter's point of view:

After stretching the net on the shore to dry beneath the rising sun, you sit to catch your breath and stare at the ground, tired after a frustrating night. In your countless times on the lake, you never failed to catch plenty of fish, but now all you have for the market is rocks and sticks.

"Did you catch anything?" Jesus is half-serious, half-smiling, as if he already knows the answer. "You should drop the net on the other side of the boat."

In this perspective, the "you" is the reader, who is Peter unnamed, experiencing the story in the right-now sense of present tense. This style is hard to write for anything other than a how-to book. Only a few people have mastered it well enough to use it in storytelling.

> Readers see themselves as the second-person "you" in the story.

One of the few good examples of second-person storytelling is *Bright Lights, Big City* by Jay McInerney. Here are his opening lines:

You are not the kind of guy who would be at a place like this at this time of the morning. But here you are, and you cannot say that the terrain is entirely unfamiliar, although the details are fuzzy. You are at a nightclub talking to a girl with a shaved head.

Third Person: a split personality is telling the story.

Grammatically, the third-person perspective that uses *he* or *she* is not the same as the person identified with *I*. It could be anyone from someone close by to God observing from Heaven above.

A deep point of view to give readers the sense of being the character shortens that distance to as little as possible, like a separate personality within the character, solely for the purpose of using *he* or *she* instead of *I*.

From Peter's point of view:

> With third-person "he" or "she," readers want to be the main character in the story.

After stretching the net on the shore to dry beneath the rising sun, Peter sat to catch his breath and stared at the ground, tired after a frustrating night. In his countless times on the lake, he never failed to catch plenty of fish, but this time all he had for the market was rocks and sticks.

"Did you catch anything?" Jesus was half-serious, half-smiling, as if he already knew the answer. "You should drop the net on the other side of the boat."

This is almost the same as what we had in first-person, but not quite. In third person, we can state Peter's name. Readers still feel close to the character when they are limited to what that character perceives at the moment, but it's not quite as intimate and heart-rending as first-person.

We have just a little more latitude to include information that isn't as tightly restricted to what the character is most concerned about. That can be helpful yet dangerous. For example, we get to state Peter's name, but that lets us easily drift into a feeling of *observing* him instead of *being* him. Be careful, because each non-essential detail will further distance readers from feeling like they are the character.

Mixed Persons: readers become a different person in different scenes.

In a movie, we have scene changes that shift focus from our hero to the villain to an approaching storm to something else. Those scenes come together, and much is left on the editing floor, to complete the picture that shows a change in more than one character.

In our stories, we are restricted to a single character in the scene. We can't tell what's happening around the corner or what someone else is planning. This creates a limitation that must be overcome if we are to show all the essential perspectives as powerfully as what movies can deliver. We accomplish that by assigning different point-of-view characters to different scenes.

> **At the beginning of a scene, make the main character obvious.**

In writing about the great draught of fish, we might set up Peter with his struggles in maintaining a business while wanting to be a follower of Jesus. But to see the struggle and feel the tension, we need to hear the wife's complaints from her point of view. John and James are in the other boat, and we want their perspective on what's happening. Let's not forget the blind man, the Pharisee, and others who experience a change from what they see Jesus do. A few of those viewpoints weaved together in a book can be as effective as a movie.

A story can have only one main character.

We can have different points-of-view by using a different main character for a scene. Every scene could be written in third-person, the only difference being who the main *he* or *she* character is for that scene. But if any of the story is to be written in first-person, that perspective should be used only for one character.

If we were to use first-person *I* for Peter's story, then he is the author of his story. All other perspectives found in other scenes show readers something important that Peter doesn't see, because it will affect him, changing who he is and what he does.

In writing your story, you don't have to use first-person at all, but if you do, use it for just one character. He doesn't have to be the main character but usually is.

When writing in third-person for your point-of-view character, some find it helpful to think in first-person and then convert to the grammatical third-person. That method might help you avoid accidentally hopping into the head of another character.

The Best Sense of Time

Writers rejoice when they can reach their audience with the right
words at the right time. — Proverbs 15:23

We have seven days in a week and twenty-four hours in a day, but
it all happens one second at a time. You anticipate what comes
next, but you can't be sure what that will actually be until the
moment gets here.

Authors can be like God.

With your great knowledge of the story, you may be able to tell all
that has happened, is happening, and will happen. Your main
character can't do that. She sees what's happening only at the
present moment. She may worry about
or anticipate the future. She will
remember only snippets from the
past—the parts that either bother her
or give her hope. She can't know all
that you know. If she did, the story wouldn't be captivating.

> **Realism in a story is
> built from the human
> perspective, not divine.**

The best way to ruin your story is to let your omniscient
knowledge creep into the narrative.

The future must always remain in doubt.

If your point-of-view character can't see it, you can't write it. You
want to avoid statements like these:

- *Little did he know how much worse things would get.*
- *This would not be the first time she would deal with that problem.*

14

- *They had never been able to break through, but they would soon find a way.*

If you want readers to anticipate a future that your character can't foresee, emphasize her confidence that something will or won't happen. The stronger the emphasis, the more that readers will anticipate the opposite happening. They'll keep reading to find out if it really does.

- *Things couldn't get worse. Absolutely not. They had to get better. He was sure of it.*
- *Finally she had the problem solved. With all she had been through, she was Superwoman, able to leap tall buildings. Nothing could get in her way now. No way.*
- *They'd tried everything. Breaking through was impossible. David might have slain Goliath, but this was like putting a sword in a toddler's hand and expecting him to defeat an army. It wasn't going to happen.*

In the first set of examples, we need only a few words to tell readers what the future holds. That's *easier*, but it's not *better*, because readers aren't challenged to anticipate what *might* happen. In real life, we often worry about what *might* happen.

> **Rewarding drama comes from not knowing what the future will be.**

The unexpected happens all the time.

Sometimes we say events are "unbelievable," because they defy the laws of probability. In conversation, saying with conviction and an honest face might convince your audience that it's true, that it really happened. But in both fiction and nonfiction, as soon as readers think, *No way. That's unbelievable,* they become disengaged. The reality of the story is ruined.

Suppose these things happen:

- *Jack stubbed his toe on a rock and uncovered the largest diamond ever found.*
- *Bill was playing poker and filled an inside straight—three times in one night.*

- *On the day Janet was fired, she met a stranger who offered her a job that made her a millionaire.*

In effective storytelling, the cavalry cannot ride in to save the day. Your character can't suddenly have skills we never knew he had. No one can be unbelievably lucky.

> **Truth has no value unless readers believe it.**

How could we make our examples more believable? We need foreshadowing where the arrival of the cavalry wasn't expected but makes perfect sense when it happens.

Circumstances leading up to winning hands become believable when readers see it as more than just "pure luck."

- *Jack was always looking, never finding. Excited rock hounds had combed the area countless times and rarely found a diamond large enough to be worth anything. Too tired to lift his feet, he tripped over himself. He looked back, picked up the rock that had stubbed his toe, and stuffed it into his pocket—a souvenir of another uneventful day.*
- *Bill knew the odds. He'd made millions playing the game to win. But this was a different kind of game, one that he would enjoy losing so his wife would have nothing to gloat about in the divorce.*
- *Escorted from the building, Janet walked toward her car, carrying the belonging she had cleared from her desk. Without a job, she held nothing of value except the picture of her daughter. "Here," she said to a well-dressed man entering the homeless camp. "Maybe you can use this stuff. I have no need for it anymore."*

The more dynamic and life-changing an outcome is to be, the more words and more time that will be needed to make it believable.

Tense Matters

God sits outside the realm of time, able to speak of the future as if it had already happened. He can speak to any point in his timeline as if it were the present, but people aren't so mobile.

Our storytelling needs to place our character in only the present moment. A different verb is used to place earlier events in history, and another verb is used to anticipate the future.

In English, we have several different senses of time available to us:

- Future: I will write my book.
- Future-perfect: I will have written my book.
- Future-progressive: I will be writing my book.
- Present: I write my book.
- Present-perfect: I have written my book.
- Present-progressive: I am writing my book.
- Simple past: I wrote my book.
- Past-progressive: I was writing my book.
- Past-perfect: I had written my book.
- Past-perfect progressive: I had been writing my book.

Each of these has a different sense of place and action in time, which need to precisely relate to where the character is at the present moment.

Time always moves forward, one moment after another.

Storytelling is most easily and effectively handled in past tense for the present moments as they unfold. Don't get the idea that you can have a bestseller just because you follow the practice of your favorite author who used present tense. Nicholas Sparks wrote *The Notebook* in simple past tense until the nursing scene at the end, where he skillfully writes in present tense.

> **Stories are usually best told in simple past tense.**

For most of us, writing is hard enough without the added challenge of maintaining the proper placement of the character in time by using present tense.

Past-tense storytelling has a "present" feel for what has happened.

Suddenly the shower turned to a downpour of hail, so heavy the windshield was solid white. He couldn't see the freeway in front of the car. He couldn't see anything behind him. At sixty miles per hour, what could he do? If he kept going, he might run off the road, hit a guard rail, or crash into someone. If he stopped, then another car would probably crash into him.

> In storytelling, "showing" means everything is happening now.

In our storytelling, we want to be cautious about the past-perfect "had" verb forms because their description of conditions or actions from a previous time can break the flow of present successive events. For example, we might add to our story:

Nothing like this had ever happened to him before.

This sentence is the voice of an observer, telling readers information that our main character knows quite well. He doesn't need the reminder. What might he do right now, which wouldn't interrupt the flow of the story?

He prayed like he had never prayed before.

Yes, we still have the "had" verb, but now we're showing what happens in the present rather than telling about the past.

Present-tense storytelling has an air of immediacy.

The actions seem indefinite, suspended in time, not yet finished. Here's what the same story might look like in present tense:

Suddenly the shower turns to a downpour of hail, so heavy the windshield is solid white. He can't see the freeway in front of the car. He can't see anything behind him. At sixty miles per hour, what can he do? If he keeps going, he could run off the road, hit a guard rail, or crash into someone. If he stops, then another car will probably crash into him.

When writing in the present tense, the previous time needs the past tense.

Nothing like this happened to him before.

Some writers will leap to a time prior to the past, as if they were writing in past tense.

Nothing like this had happened to him before.

This is where present-tense writing can become really tricky. The next thing we know, the author is drifting in and out of present, past perfect, and also past tense, so readers aren't sure where they are in time. Consistency is especially challenging. To remain in the present sense of time, we might use a sentence like this:

He prays like never before.

Sentences need to move forward.

Some people think passive voice is to be avoided at all cost. That's not true. You want to avoid it when it's not the best choice.

What is "passive voice"? Most commonly, you may see it defined as the use of the state-of-being verbs such as *is, am, was*, and *were*. However, grammatical structure doesn't own the final vote on what constitutes "passive." The best definition is "not active." That is, nothing is *happening* now, moving the story forward. Readers want John to do something, not be told that something exists or something was done.

> Readers want to go, not wait, and to run, not walk.

You may have heard that passive voice is *telling*, not *showing*, which we would never want to do, right? Not necessarily. Telling is essential and becomes showing when readers feel a desperate need for the information.

What is often regarded as passive can be the correct visual of an ongoing action. For example:

John stood.

That's an accurate description of someone sitting at the table and moving to a standing position. But it would not be accurate to write:

John stood in the corner.

Not when he was already there, standing. And a minute later, he's still standing there. It would be correct to say:

John was standing.

Use of the past-perfect verbs using "had" are passive when they have the sense of pointing toward something that has already happened. Since we want to keep our stories moving forward with the action, we must be careful to use "had" only in the present sense.

Grammar-checking software may give you a bad grade for what may actually be good writing. Or vice-versa. What you should be looking for are places where the story or message topic doesn't move forward in time.

> **Be smart with your writing, because you can't always trust the "experts" to be right.**

When the subject of the sentence *receives* action instead of *giving* it, we have passive voice. But it could still have an active sense. Sometimes we know the effect and either don't want to reveal or don't know the cause. For example:

The ball was caught.

We don't know who threw it. Maybe it was John. That's the mystery, and we need mystery, tension, and suspense.

Some writers think –ing verbs must always be avoided, that they are a sign of weak writing. Many times, they are, but not always.

"The King of Ing" was written to illustrate how unnecessary those verbs might be:

At dawn, the of King of Ing was standing at his window, wishing for a better way of communicating with his people who were not responding to his commanding style but were sitting, resting, and accomplishing little.

He started pacing, moving from one side of the room to the other, contemplating what to do. Knowing improvement was not happening without something changing, he was considering acquiring a differing way of writing. Therefore, using his own quill, he began composing an edict for posting at the city square.

Besides the king's name, twenty-two words end with *ing*, and they can all be avoided.

At dawn, the King of Ing stood at his window and wished for a better way to communicate with his people who had not responded to his commands but sat, rested, and accomplished little. As he paced from one side of the room to the other, he contemplated what to do. Without change, improvement is impossible, so he considered a different way to write. Therefore, he used his own quill to compose this edict posted at the city square: Your leader has decided to speak in better style as your new King of Simple Past Tense.

We want to minimize their use, but not avoid them altogether, not when they create the more accurate picture of a necessarily ongoing action. Unless it's a sudden burst, the wind doesn't just blow. It is blowing.

The bottom line: keep the story moving forward. And perhaps one of the best ways to do that is not to worry about passive voice.

Look for what will keep the story moving.

Let clauses flow with the times.

Reactions follow action, effects follow causes, and conclusions come as the result of something. One thought leads

> **What happens first needs to come first.**

to another. Everything that happens follows whatever preceded it. Since that's the way life happens, that's the order we should see on the page.

When something happens that doesn't make sense, we've missed showing the cause. You don't want readers thinking, *That's strange. I wonder why that happened.* When the explanation follows, we're too late. We've already begun to disengage the reader.

Watch for trailing clauses that begin with *after* or *because.*

- *Johnny went out to play after cleaning up his room.*
- *We need to get home, because a storm is coming.*
- *"Don't do it," Tina screamed, when the man looked ready to jump.*
- *Suzie locked the door and closed the blinds after hearing that a killer had been seen in her neighborhood.*

Johnny had to clean his room first. Then he could go out to play. First the weather alert, then came the need to get home. Why did Tina scream? We need to see the cause before the effect, even when they happen at almost the same time. If Susie was looking out the window and saw someone she thought was the killer, what would her order of actions be?

- *Get a knife from the kitchen drawer.*
- *Close the living room blinds.*
- *Hide in the bedroom closet.*
- *Lock the front door.*
- *Call 9-1-1.*
- *Find her cell phone.*

Susie might do all these things, but definitely not in this order. Analyze every clause and sentence to be sure one thing naturally leads to the next.

Actions need to precede the results.

Misplaced actions are like watching a movie when the sound and video are out of sync.

- *"You have a beautiful redbud tree blooming outside your window." Catherine opened the curtains.*
- *Patricia took his plate of food to him. She had added a couple of tomato slices to give it some color.*
- *"Is this seat taken?" Bill motioned toward the empty chair.*

Catherine can't remark about the beauty until after she draws back the curtains and sees the tree. Since the tomato slices came before the plate was delivered, we need that information first. Bill wouldn't ask if the seat was taken, then motion toward it a few seconds later.

- *Catherine opened the curtains. "You have a beautiful redbud tree blooming outside your window."*
- *Patricia added a couple of tomato slices for color and took his plate of food to him.*
- *Bill motioned toward the empty chair. "Is this seat taken?"*

Place words and phrases near what they modify.

We have a picture in mind when we write, but if our words aren't in the right order, readers can become confused or have the wrong picture.

> A writing mistake is a bad way to make a reader laugh.

- *Sam sold his dune buggy to a neighbor with chrome wheels.*
- *Please take time to discuss the proposal that is attached with your wife.*
- *Washed and waxed, Jim proudly drove his new car.*
- *William gulped a steaming cup of coffee before leaving for work.*

Readers move from left to right, word by word, as they create a mental image. Was the cup steaming, or was it the coffee? A neighbor with chrome wheels, a wife attached to a proposal, and a man who is washed and waxed aren't the kinds of pictures we want our readers to create.

- *Sam sold his dune chrome-wheeled buggy to a neighbor.*
- *Please take time to discuss with your wife the attached proposal.*
- *Jim proudly drove his new car, washed and waxed.*
- *Before leaving for work, William gulped a steaming cup of coffee.*

Finding the Best Story

You are expressly purposed through our ministry to be Jesus' letter to the world—not written with pen and ink but by the Spirit of our living God. His message will not be read from stone tablets but from your changed hearts. — 2 Corinthians 3:3

News tells what happens. That's boring. But story is different. Instead of *telling* what happens, story should make readers want to *find out* what happens.

A story must be engaging.

We engage readers with an upfront sense that something has gone wrong or soon will. They must believe they will be entertained, educated, or encouraged. If they think a movie or TV show will do better, they won't spend time reading.

> **Know what's most important and make it more important.**

In everyday life, people try to avoid tension, confrontation, and tragedy. But the struggle is always there when they want something and can't get it. So to make our stories real and engaging, we must constantly strive to identify the tension, confrontation, and tragedy that will hold our readers' attention.

Stories have a beginning, middle, and end.

A garden hose has a beginning, middle, and end, but it's not a story. So does a football game and a church service. But those aren't stories either. To have a story, we must have characters who experience unexpected pleasures and pains that change their lives for better or worse.

At the beginning, something has gone wrong or is about to.

During the middle, the struggle escalates as matters get worse.

In the end, the joy of victory or the agony of defeat shows a significant change in character and reveals something important about life.

If your main character is the same at the end as she is in the beginning, you don't have a story.

The beginning content is crucial.

Disengage readers at the beginning, and they'll never venture through the middle and reach the reward at the end. Bore them with description that isn't essential to your main character's concerns, and only the committed reader will keep turning the pages.

The setup in the beginning should give readers just enough information for them to identify who they are in the scene, where they are, and what they want.

> **The start is your first and maybe your only chance to make a good impression.**

Picture the situation as clearly as possible. Be the main character and ask, what do I want? Why am I worried about what will happen next? What am I anticipating that is important to me? Without significant concerns, readers aren't concerned.

Think about your personal story.

At the beginning, did you know how your personal experience would end? No, you might have thought you did, but the journey always has many unexpected twists and turns that are easily forgotten.

At the end, you might say, "I knew that was going to happen," but think about that for a while. Go back to what you first expected and notice what you were worried about and what went wrong. And then there's what went right, but you didn't expect it to happen that way.

The more you think about your story, the more you'll see the contrast, how much different the end was from the beginning. Then you should realize that in the beginning, you really didn't know what the end would be. That's the way we must begin our story, worrying about what will happen next. You aren't sure how it will end.

At the beginning, if readers are able to sense the end, you don't have a story.

Outlines can be your worst enemy.

One of the worst things we learned in school is the importance of an outline.

Not only is an outline not important, it's self-defeating. Characters are forced into actions they wouldn't naturally choose, and crucial elements that would make a character's choices believable are often missed. Why? Because a character's choices are naturally driven by what they desire and the obstacles they face, not what an outline says needs to happen.

> **Bad outlines don't help a story.**

If you want a great outline, write it after your story is finished.

Story happens now, not in backstory.

Jesus said that looking back from the plow leaves people unfit for the Kingdom of God (Luke 9:62). When our stories keep looking back to tell what happened earlier, they are unfit for the kingdom of best storytellers.

Time spent revealing the past is a U-turn that drives readers in the wrong direction. But wait, aren't the memories of our past an important, sometimes essential, part of our current concerns as we drive forward? Yes, they are, but they need to be present thoughts as we focus on the road ahead. Too much staring at the rearview mirror will crash your story.

A start in the present with a turn to backstory:

Charlie swerved right, then took a sharp turn to the left, down the alley. Flashing red lights were still on his tail. The last time he was chased by the police, he jerked to the side to avoid one car and crashed into another. He was caught, handcuffed, and spent six months in jail. He should have paid better attention. If only he had gone the other way, he wouldn't be in such a mess now.

The same paragraph in the present:

Charlie swerved right, then took a sharp turn to the left, down the alley. Flashing red lights were still on his tail. He couldn't afford to avoid one car ahead, only to crash into another. No more handcuffs. No more time in jail. No more making the same mistakes. This time he had to find a way out and avoid an even bigger mess.

In the second example, present thoughts tell readers all they need to know about the past. He was handcuffed, spent time in jail, and made foolish choices. But now we haven't damaged the forward movement of the story by looking back to what happened after a previous car chase.

> **Plots driven by the character are better than characters driven by a plot.**

After a captivating start, don't lose reader interest in the middle.

The strength of any story is the struggle in the middle, which must take your main character from who he was to who he will be. Don't assume that readers will care like you do. Give them no choice by facing obstacles and having to make decisions and take actions that matter to them.

Something must happen that makes escape seem impossible. If the problem can be avoided, readers will wonder why your character doesn't retreat.

Jesus said, "Your heart is where your treasure is." For something to go wrong, let your character lose the treasure he values most, let him visualize the treasure but make it impossible to reach, or that his greatest fear fall upon him and be desperate to escape.

Why do readers lose interest in the boring middle?

- They are not entertained.
- They think the climax has already been reached.
- They aren't worried about what will happen next.
- They don't care about the character.
- Repetition and redundancy reminds them of what they already know.
- They can't picture the scene.

Story is not something we should build from a blueprint.

Develop your story from a need that leads to asking the right questions and pursuing answers that often don't work.

When the choices are easy, we have a weak story. Choosing between a good thing and a bad thing isn't much of a choice. Let your reader choose between two bad things. Or let your reader choose the bad instead of the good, because he thinks he has no choice.

> **An unpredictable life can't happen from a blueprint.**

What's real in our writing world is different from real life.

Unexplainable coincidences and unbelievable results happen all the time. But in storytelling, events must make sense and be believable.

Our lives may seem to be unfolding haphazardly, but our storytelling needs a cohesive thread from one thing to what readers think would naturally follow. Our minds may be filled with questions needing answers, but our readers will be very disappointed if we leave them hanging, without answers.

The all-important middle must build to an all-rewarding end.

The end marks a new beginning.

When you get to the end, you may see a need to rewrite the beginning. You can now tweak the weak places in the all-important middle. Why? Because you know your story better, and you can see ways to make readers more concerned at the beginning. And you can add even more tension to the struggles.

> The end is the best place to start making good writing great.

You now know your characters better than you know yourself. How have they changed? What have they learned? They now have a new outlook on life. What is it? In the final scene, we need to see that picture in action.

Seven Essential Storytelling Blocks

Pray for the publishing of God's message, so it will be honored among others as it has been in you. — *1 Thessalonians 3:1*

In English classes, students are taught the importance of having an outline before writing the story. Outlining is important for nonfiction presentation of facts, history, and news in general. But for storytelling? Not a good idea, because characters become molded plastic, forced to conform to what the author wants to happen, not what the character would naturally do.

What works best for readers and the most natural way for us to write takes us into the character, and we see what happens. True to life, one thing will lead to another as the main character survives the struggle, learns an important lesson, and is changed.

> **Aimless writing is sure to take readers nowhere special.**

The danger is allowing your main character to wander aimlessly.

If the character in your story doesn't seem to be going anywhere meaningful, having no apparent need or desire, readers will lose patience because they can't enjoy the feeling of a purposeless life for very long.

Seven important elements of story are essential.

To hold a reader's attention, we can get help from the SCOOP IT UP acronym. Instead of an outline, we just need to be sure we have the most crucial parts of story covered. Obviously, character would be one of them. Without a character to care about, we don't have much of a story, but that's not all. To reward readers with as much as what they get on the movie screen, we need a tight focus on all seven areas through each scene, chapter, and book. Without those building blocks, we deprive readers of the strong feeling for what's happening now—and they won't have much concern for what comes next. Here are the seven blocks that we will soon cover in greater depth:

> **Before you start, know where you're headed.**

- **S**ituation . . . puts readers into the scene at a particular time and place.
- **C**haracter . . . pulls readers into the situation with a reason to care what happens.
- **O**bjective . . . gives the story a sense of purpose, to move the action forward and make readers care what will happen next.
- **O**bstacles . . . put the outcome in doubt so readers will keep turning the pages to find out what tragedy or triumph will follow.
- **P**light . . . reveals the great consequence of your character's success or failure in reaching the objective.
- **I**nsight & **T**ransformation . . . shows the important lesson learned that results in a change in the character.
- **U**nresolved **P**roblem . . . points to the next great concern.

Your story must be captivating.

Christian writers are more about the message than the money. Sometimes they say they want to "change the world." That is best accomplished by holding readers' interest through life-changing experiences shown in a story. As they see themselves in the character's situation, they are taught by the experience.

Experience is the best teacher.

Many centuries ago, Plato urged the city fathers of Athens to exile storytellers. Was he serious? Yes, he was. Here's why he said storytelling should be banned:

> *Every captivating story sends a charged idea out to us, in effect compelling the idea into us, so that we must believe.* — *Plato, 388 BC*

Plato thought storytellers were dangerous people. Was he right? Your story should not be built from the pressures of life, not a blueprint. Let it develop from a need that leads to asking the right questions and pursuing answers that often don't work.

Your stories must be "real."

Many people detest horror stories. Some don't want to read intense suspense. Why? Because what happens in those stories is so real, they feel the danger as if they were there.

You're the writer. You get to decide how much tension, terror, and tragedy will be included in your story.

Beware the Christian tendency to avoid tension and conflict and write as if life is wonderful. There will always be a happy ending. Our trust in God will not allow anything to go wrong. That approach represents life that isn't real, and it won't help readers cope with the conflicts and trauma they face all the time.

> **Without the struggle, victory is meaningless.**

When you focus on the most fundamental needs of story—situation, character, objective, obstacle, and plight, and you look forward to the insight and transformation and unresolved problem—you'll sense what needs to happen in each scene to drive your story forward.

Whether fiction or nonfiction, stories should read the same.

Great nonfiction stories have the same SCOOP IT UP elements as fiction, with a character in desperate need, facing obstacles that put the outcome in doubt. In fiction, you get to imagine what those things are and write them in a way that readers would swear it's all true. In nonfiction, you're challenged to imagine the situation as it really was, recognize the character's desperate need, and identify the obstacles that put the outcome in doubt. Sounds the same, doesn't it? And it is, just in a slightly different way.

Nonfiction storytellers sometimes think they can't include elements in the story that lack proof of what happened or was said. For example, throughout the life of Christ, we have no mention of rain. We hear of wind and waves. No rain. Does that mean it never rained? Of course not. Weather existed on every day of Jesus' walk on Earth, so to leave out that element in our stories, just because the Bible doesn't say so, damages the truth instead of helping it.

> **Without the details, we have insufficient evidence to believe a nonfiction story is true.**

In nonfiction storytelling, we want to fill the gaps between what we know with what we can't know but must assume in order to make readers feel like they are there, experiencing the same tension and conflict. Call it "speculative nonfiction," if you like, but the goal is the same for both fiction and nonfiction with some fictionalization.

Both must be believable, or we don't have a story.

Situation

*Respecting God's ability above your own, humble
yourselves, and God will cause your writing effort
to prosper in due time. — 1 Peter 5:6*

The *situation* puts readers into the scene at a particular time and place. Before readers can experience a scene, they must have a picture in mind.

We need only enough information for readers not to feel lost. Make the situation interesting, but keep the description short. This is the *before* condition that will be remarkably and memorably different from the *after*.

> **Time and place must be clear, or readers will feel lost.**

There was a time when you could spend a page describing landscape and weather. Not anymore. Kill the setup and as quickly as possible get to the main character who has a desperate need. Those opening lines may be the most important sentences you write. They set the tone and reader expectation for what is to follow.

To get started, don't create a forest fire. Just light a match.

Opening lines become great when they have . . .

- A question that demands an answer.
- A shock factor, introducing an unexpected perspective.
- Something humorous or entertaining, which invites pursuit of reading pleasure.

34

- An emotional hook, prompting concern for what will happen next.
- A sense of adventure, stirring curiosity over what important lesson might be learned.
- The lighting of a fuse that points to explosive moments ahead.

Your opening lines may be your first and only chance to grab reader interest.

In both fiction and nonfiction, stories may be poorly written and have weak plots, but they *should* always have great opening lines. You can use the "look inside" feature of Amazon-listed books to read any number of first paragraphs and learn from them. Pick a few that grab your attention, and copy what was written.

Evaluate each one. Some little-known books have great openings while bestsellers might not. Did the first paragraph make you want to keep reading? Why? How did it set the tone for what might follow? Can you think of words that might be better? If this approach were used in your story, how would you reword it?

> **Study great writing with a goal to become even better.**

Reading other writers' great openings will improve your feel for what might work best in your story. Take time to rewrite those openings in your own words, and you'll do even better.

Here are some opening lines:

1984 by George Orwell

It was a bright, cold day in April, and the clocks were striking thirteen. Winston Smith, his chin nuzzled into his breast in an effort to escape the vile wind, slipped quickly through the glass doors of Victory Mansions, though not quickly enough to prevent a swirl of gritty dust from entering along with him.

A Tale of Two Cities by Charles Dickens

It was the best of times, it was the worst of times, it was the age of wisdom, it was the age of foolishness, it was the epoch of belief, it was the epoch of incredulity, it was the season of Light, it was the season of Darkness, it was the spring of hope, it was the winter of despair, we had everything before us, we had nothing before us, we were all going direct to Heaven, we were all going direct the other way—in short, the period was so far like the present period, that some of its noisiest authorities insisted on its being received, for good or for evil, in the superlative degree of comparison only.

Adventures in Darkness by **Tom Sullivan**

Ja-Jing—Step, Step.
Ja-Jing—Step, Step.
Ja-Jing—Step, Step.

I listened to the syncopated rhythms of the fat man as he patrolled the echoing halls of the boarding school, my personal prison. The sound of his leather-soled shoes and heavy key ring framed his every movement, and I knew exactly where he was throughout his nightly rounds. My escape, planned so carefully, was about to begin. Though I was nervous—even a little frightened—the freedom on the other side of the walls was far more important to me than any consequence I might suffer for what I was about to do.

> **What works inside the story will often come from outside the box.**

Breaking Dawn by **Stephenie Meyer**

No one is staring at you, I promised myself. No one is staring at you. No one is staring at you.

But, because I couldn't lie convincingly even to myself, I had to check.

Forrest Gump by **Winston Groom**

Let me say this: bein a idiot is no box of chocolates. People laugh, lose patience, treat you shabby. Now they says folks sposed to be kind to the afflicted, but let me tell you— it ain't always that way. Even so, I got no complaints, cause I reckon I done live a pretty interestin life, so to speak.

From Birth to Seven by Carole A. Bell

We've all found ourselves scanning the rows of books in a store or surfing the web, looking for parenting answers. We settle on one or more books and make our purchases. We try to do what the books say, but we still want to strangle the kid.

Plant My Feet by Duane Griffith

Drops of water poured from my skin as the sun radiated straight down. A stiff southwest breeze pushed against me. The noontime was hot, but on this day in April 1891, the heat I felt did not come from the sun.

Pride and Prejudice by Jane Austen

It is a truth universally acknowledged, that a single man in possession of a good fortune, must be in want of a wife.

Testaments by Margaret Atwood

Only dead people are allowed to have statues, but I have been given one while still alive. Already I am petrified.

The Adventures of Huckleberry Finn by Mark Twain

You don't know about me without you have read a book by the name of *The Adventures of Tom Sawyer;* but that ain't no matter. That book was made by Mr. Mark Twain, and he told the truth, mainly. There was things which he stretched, but mainly he told the truth. That is nothing. I never seen anybody but lied one time or another, without it was Aunt Polly, or the widow, or maybe Mary. Aunt Polly–Tom's Aunt Polly, she is– and Mary, and the Widow Douglas is all told about in that book, which is mostly a true book, with some stretchers, as I said before.

> The number-rule for creativity says there is no rule.

The Girl on the Train by Paula Hawkins

I'm on the 8:04, but I'm not going into London. I'm going to Witney instead. I'm hoping that being there will jog my memory, that I'll get to the station and I'll see everything clearly, I'll know. I don't hold out much hope, but there is nothing else I can do. I can't call Tom. I'm too ashamed, and in any case, he's made it clear: he wants nothing more to do with me.

The Queen by **Steven James**

Kirk Tyler turned the computer monitor to face his captive.

The Voyage of the 'Dawn Treader' by **C. S. Lewis**

There was a boy called Eustace Clarence Scrubb, and he almost deserved it. His parents called him Eustace Clarence and masters called him Scrubb. I can't tell you how his friends spoke to him, for he had none.

Think of the situation from your main character's point of view.

As the main character, ask, "Who am I? Where am I? What do I want? Why am I concerned?" Your answers should not be based on who she will be or who you know she is, but on who she thinks she is at the beginning. Include just enough about the scene for readers to feel like they know where they are, like walking into a familiar room in which all that matters is what's important to her.

> **Find the best answers by asking more questions.**

Character

If I speak with human excellence and angelic might yet don't really care for the wellbeing of those I serve, my message is like a noisy gong or clanging cymbal, getting attention but not really helping. — *1 Corinthians 13:1*

Your main character in a scene pulls readers into the situation with a reason to care what happens. They may love the character or hate him. He may be seen as a hero, villain, or stranger walking down the street. Whoever he is, one thing is crucial: readers must have a good reason to care.

Clearly define your point-of-view character.

Time, place, and situation are important at the beginning of every scene, but nothing can be more important than making readers identify with the scene's main character. Make that person obvious right away, hopefully in the first sentence but definitely in the first paragraph. This is especially crucial when a new scene changes the point-of-view character.

> Readers are lost when they don't know who they are in the story.

Have your character use internal dialog or describe a physical sensation that only your character, not an observer, could have. Avoid describing landscape and weather, but let a few of those details show readers where the character is.

Avoid the *telling* verbs.

When readers move from the observer position to being the character, they would seldom describe themselves with clauses such as *he thought, she considered,* or *he wondered.* Watch for verbs like *knew, believed,* or *contemplated.* Even *saw, heard,* and *felt* are to be avoided if possible. Go directly to the character's observation of what was seen, heard, or felt, without using those verbs.

Here are statements that *observe* our character:

- She wondered what the next step should be.
- He thought he would never face that problem again.
- He believed everything would be all right.
- She watched the car race by at ninety miles per hour.

How can we convert those statements to *being* the character?

- What should the next step be?
- He will never face that problem again.
- Everything was going to be all right.
- The car raced by at ninety miles per hour.

Know what people love and hate.

The difference between the hero and the villain is the percentage of good and bad qualities. Good people have flaws and bad people have virtues. Think about what you like and dislike about your main character in a scene. Then give readers a reason to care by revealing some of his good and bad traits through his dialog and actions.

> Strive to make readers laugh or cry—and be uncomfortable anywhere in between.

We can't know people without spending time with them. To make your story believable, you must know your characters by spending lots of time with them, following them and doing what they do. Find out what they love and hate, what they like and what they dislike:

- Love the underdog.

- Hate deceivers who take advantage of others.
- Want to be loved and appreciated.
- Love people with spunk, spirit, and passion.
- Want people to succeed against impossible odds.
- Care for those who face problems like we have.
- Identify with people who are confused and are struggling to find their way.
- Dislike those who are stubborn and won't accept facts or listen to reason.
- Love freedom and hate bondage.
- Like people with a good sense of humor.
- Care for those who make mistakes but want to change.
- Don't like self-centered, sensitive, uncaring people.
- Like people who support our goals and dislike those who stand in our way.

Reveal the point-of-view character.

In the days when photo film had to be developed, the person holding the camera was never in the picture. Today, we need to understand that in our best-writing world, selfies are not allowed.

You may think readers need to know more about your main character's appearance, but that's not true from her point of view. When she walks into a conference room, she is looking at everyone else, not herself.

> An engaging story requires the right perspective.

Show her concern as she walks into the room:

She took the chair farthest from the CEO, sat straight, and pulled the hair back from her eyes.

Avoid adding details that an observer might notice but your character has no reason to care about.

She took the black padded conference chair on the far end of the long mahogany conference table, farthest from the CEO, sat straight, and pulled back her long flowing red hair from her pretty blue eyes.

Don't laugh. You'll see such descriptions of main characters in bestselling novels, but that doesn't make it the best writing.

Avoid using a mirror to reveal your character's appearance. That trick has been overdone and usually appears contrived. If it's really important, let others say something about your main character's appearance that prompts a reaction.

"Susan, what did you do to your hair?"
    She fluffed the tight curls and smiled. "Do you like it? The straight blonde look was so ordinary. I'll have more fun as a redhead."

Be careful. The question must be a perfect fit for the scene and not appear manipulated to reveal information for the readers that isn't the character's concern.

> **To write the fatal distraction, include details that aren't crucial.**

Point-of-view characters never need to describe the color of their eyes, the nature of their smiles, or how they look when walking down the street. When readers want to see how they look, they will fill in that part of the picture from their own imaginations, and that's better.

Hold tightly to your main character's point of view.

Leaving your main character's perspective to give readers information, even for a moment, jerks your audience away from the action to be an observer of what doesn't matter.

In real life, how do characters receive crucial information? It happens through phone calls, texts, or letters. Radio, television, or online resources are accessed to the extent that your main character needs to know. In dialog, you can reveal all kinds of things that wouldn't otherwise be known. Just make sure the information fits the situation in which there is a need to know.

First create the need.

Information exists everywhere, and it's boring—the best way to put your readers to sleep.

You always want your information to connect with your characters' feelings and desires. If your character in the story doesn't have a need for the information, then readers have to detach themselves from the characters to know something from the storyteller. Can you see how destructive that might be?

> Readers are bored with details when they feel no need to know.

A story must have a character caught in desperate want of something that people care about. In pursuit of that desire, obstacles reveal their nature, teach something, and bring about change. Without that, we have no story, just news.

Weave the details subtly into the action of the story.

Readers will naturally adjust their imagination of the character as actions reveal more details. If she can't reach the top shelf, we know something about her height. If he has to duck to walk through the door, we see someone who could dunk a basketball without leaping.

Since people habitually compare themselves with others, your-point-of-view character could compare herself with the competition. Just be sure the need for that comparison is clear in the scene.

Remember that the character cannot see herself. You can't say her face turned red, because she can't see that. Maybe her skin crawled or her cheeks heated, because she can sense that. Her eyes filling with tears sounds too much like the perspective of an outside observer. Let her do something like squinting to subdue the tears or swallowing hard trying to say something.

Characters have character that must be shown.

Most body language exists without conscious thought. To maintain a captivating perspective, you can only describe what your character wants to see at that moment. In another situation, she might be aware of her shortness of breath, but maybe not now.

Sounds and smells are most often neglected. The first step the description is usually what we see, and then we tell how we felt. There is a better way. Think hard on the sounds and odors of your character's surroundings. Do your best to avoid telling how your character feels. Lead your readers to the feeling through hearing and smelling and then show the reaction with as little interpretation as possible.

> How people act and what they do means more than what they say.

Take advantage of words that create a feeling of sound, like squeaking doors, buzzing insects, and creaking stairs. Movies give you the sounds. To compete, you must create those sounds, but don't overdo the special effects.

Body language reveals character.

Don't tell readers that your character was angry. Show it by revealing what the anger looked like in actions, expressions, and tone of voice. You want to move beyond simple smiles and tears and describe the expressions, posture, and actions that reveal your character. You will find a wealth of ideas in Appendix section "Expressions, Posture, and Actions."

Be careful with these ideas. You can use them in description of a point-of-view character's actions, but never use them in observation of the character. Your main character can see others in this way, but she cannot see herself.

Male and female personalities are different.

Some in our society might thing we should be basically alike, but the truth is, we're all basically different. The male and female physique is significantly different, and so are the thought patterns and behaviors.

In general, men use logic more than feeling. They tend to prefer adventure over security. They like mechanics and solving problems. They pursue goals, increase their self-worth through achievements, and love their tools. They are more likely to sense direction relevant to north, south, east, and west. They notice women, the speed with which things move, and measure strength and weakness from a physical perspective.

On the other hand, women are more concerned with the feeling than whether something makes sense. They love comfort and protection and are not as interested in taking risks when they can be avoided. Their feeling of self-worth depends more on positive feedback from others, and flowers are more important than tools. They are special in their sense of direction, thinking more in terms of knowing whether they should turn right or left. They notice people's expressions, the color of a person's eyes, and how people are dressed. They are concerned about how others feel and are sensitive to a person's tone as much as the words.

Be aware of those differences as you write about the opposite sex, because they should be much different from who you are. Our weakest writing comes from sensing and interpreting a character's surroundings the same as we perceive our world.

Forget the character charts.

Character charts present the same difficulty as outlines. They can force your character into speaking and acting in unnatural ways, merely to conform to the chart's requirement. Life is much too complicated and variable to outline in a chart.

A chart can be beneficial in identifying characters' histories—their background, education, social status, beliefs, and achievements—but that has little to do with the future, how your character will

> **What characters do is often unpredictable and unplannable.**

change in response to the dangers ahead and everything that will go wrong.

You know their past? Great. Put that behind you where it belongs and move forward with what is happening to your character now.

Recognize situational differences.

People think, talk, and act differently at different ages and different decades. They may also think, talk, and act differently after a significant event such as pregnancy, loss of a loved one, a promotion, or some natural disaster or physical threat.

Any two characters who observe the same thing will see them differently. Any one character who observes the same thing at different times will see them differently. Past events viewed in the present will seem better or worse than they were, depending on the current pleasure or plight.

Each character has a different language and desire.

Great writers become skilled at being entirely different people in different situations and times. No two people think alike, talk alike, or act alike. People have different goals and different worldviews. Each person has his own "truth" in contrast to what others believe. Even the best of friends don't always agree.

> Characters should be as predictable as the weather.

Because we know ourselves so well, we most easily have our characters think, talk, and behave like we do. Keep working on a scene until you see it clearly through the eyes of your main character, not yourself. New insights may require re-visiting previous scenes that build toward this moment.

Be sure the scene affects your character.

Scenes are small pictures within the panorama of the full story. By the end of each scene, something must change or your story has stagnated. Try to make each scene's conclusion unexpected and inevitable, a precursor to what must come next.

If your character isn't affected in some way, either positively or negatively, the scene has no right to exist. Why? Without change, we have only information that has failed in its mission to propel life forward.

The Bible says, "As the years passed, Jesus grew physically and spiritually, enjoying the favor of God and the people" (Luke

2:52). That's all we know from Scripture. Really? Jesus grew up. His Father in Heaven was pleased. The people liked him. For a story, we need much more.

Without objectives, obstacles, and plight, we have information that isn't enough to make a story. In the eighteen years after Jesus' parents found him in the Temple, we might suppose that everything was wonderful. Nothing ever went wrong. There was never a conflict. And without those things, we have no story.

Objective

Fellow writers, I've not yet become the best I can be, but I know one thing: I need to put past failures and successes behind me and focus on doing much better in the future. — Philippians 3:13

Every scene and chapter needs a sense of purpose, to move the action forward and make readers care what will happen next. You must identify the objectives—the goals—or your narrative won't be compelling, lacking a feeling that your character is going somewhere worthwhile.

If your character isn't going anywhere, neither are your readers.

Different strokes are for different folks.

Your point of view character has special interests. What are they? As an author, you might love gardening. You naturally notice the flowers and weeds. Are you an attorney, computer programmer, or a homeless person sleeping in your car that's out of gas? A clear understanding of the character's situation leads to the natural question: *What does my character want?*

> Characters always want something, but they don't always know what it is.

Readers can't cheer for someone or want his defeat if they don't know or don't care about what he is trying to accomplish.

You may have heard that action drives a story forward, we have action, reaction, evaluation, and further action. But none of that has any meaning unless the purpose, or objective, behind the action is clear to the reader.

Know what your characters want.

People always want something, but they don't always know what it is. If they think they know, they are going to be wrong to some extent. If that's not the case, then your story will be predictable and boring.

Your hero might tell you that he doesn't care—he doesn't have an objective—but he really does. Even suicide is caring so much for escape that he is willing to die for that objective. Why would he contemplate suicide? Because he cares—and readers will too.

In your character's situation in this right-now moment, your job is to determine what your character is after, even when he's not aware of his objective.

Subconscious actions reveal natural desires.

Your character will often act without thinking, which is based upon who she is, how she sees herself, or what she wants to be.

> A character's surprising action must come unannounced.

As a writer following your character's emotional journey, you might have an idea of where she's headed in the long run. But as the story unfolds and weaves through many unexpected twists and turns, the odds of your being exactly right shouldn't be very good.

We have external and internal objectives.

Like a dog chasing a car, nipping at the tires until the car stops, your character gets what he wants and will often come away with the same unfulfilled feeling that he had before. When that happens—where the achievement of his goal fails to satisfy his desires—we know that his external objective didn't meet his internal objective.

What the character says and does must match the character's personality and interests. External objectives are physically definable and reachable by some kind of action. He wants to be a millionaire. She wants to be a stay-at-home mom with three kids, two boys and a girl. He wants to own his own company. She wants to learn to play golf. An external objective is a sought-after trophy, something to own, something to be achieved.

Every external objective has a motivation behind it that will reveal the internal objective if you ask your character the right questions. Why does he want to be a millionaire? Why does she care about golf? Then answers tend to come in the form of another physical goal. He wants to be financially independent. She wants to get out of housework for a while.

> **All meaningful journeys have important goals.**

Keep drilling down with *why?* questions until the answer reveals a person's self-worth, how they feel about themselves. He wants to be a millionaire to prove he's not the worthless person his dad said he would be. She wants to be admired among the socially elite and kill the feeling that she would never be good enough.

Your characters probably won't know their internal objectives. Even if they do, their knowing won't mean much until their pursuits of external objectives prove or disprove their worth. But if you can identify their internal objectives, you'll do better at describing what matters most in the story.

What are some external goals?

- Become someone great.
- Find the treasure.
- Defeat an enemy.
- Justice or revenge.
- Avoid starvation.
- Escape a threat.
- Win someone's love.
- Reach a destination.
- Defend a loved one.
- Pursue a dream.
- End a nightmare.
- Save the world.

What are some internal goals?

- Be loved and appreciated.
- Gain respect among peers.
- Prove self-worth.
- Forgiveness and to make things right.
- Be admired as a hero.
- Overcome fear.
- Become a better person.
- Be the best at something.

Ask what your characters want.

When we're focused on what happens, we can easily miss what is most important: what the character wants at that moment. Ask your character. You might be surprised at the answer you get. What does she want in this situation? She's stuck. How can she get out of this mess? Should she run or fight? What is the last thing she would consider doing? Why might she have no choice but do it anyway?

> Interesting plot twists come from characters doing what the author least expected.

Weak writing results from a failure to ask these kinds of questions.

Obstacles

My dear storytellers, don't be unduly alarmed by the fiery ordeals that come to test your writing ability, as if this were an abnormal experience. — 1 Peter 4:12

We must put the outcome in doubt so readers will keep turning the pages to find out what tragedy or triumph will follow. Obstacles are the opposing forces that make that happen. If nothing stands in the way of what the main character wants, the story's outcome is obvious and boring.

If Solomon were speaking to writers, instead of saying, "There's nothing new under the sun," he would say, "There are no new plots." All plots have a character who wants something and is challenged by seemingly insurmountable obstacles. How wise of him to notice the sameness. He stopped short of noticing the differences in the objectives and obstacles that cause everything under the sun to be new.

> We need only a hill to have something to climb.

We need the tension that obstacles create.

Unfulfilled desires create tension, and tension is the force that propels the story forward. Behind all unfulfilled desires are obstacles that must be identified before our narrative can have the tension it needs.

In writing nonfiction, you must visualize what took place and identify what the obstacles are. Remember, without a storm, a "beautiful day" has little meaning. So often, Christians want to write about the pleasure of knowing the Lord and miss the story found in the obstacles that must be overcome to get there.

In writing fiction, you can let your imagination run wild to create whatever would make the story more captivating. Fiction opens the doors to reveal the truth in powerful ways, but only if you can imagine true-to-life obstacles that make the story real.

When people read the first pages of your story, they believe the reward will justify their time. Just telling what happened won't be good enough. Don't miss the obstacles that make your character's experience important.

Obstacles keep characters from taking the comfortable "line of least resistance."

People are forced to make a choice when they face obstacles. Do they press on or quit? Should they fight or flee? There are benefits and consequences either way. Which will it be? That question keeps readers engaged, wanting to find out if the choice was the right one.

Or will a greater obstacle follow? It must, because if the tension doesn't escalate, it deescalates. The final burst of light comes after the darkest moment. Until then, one

> **Comfortable characters put readers to sleep.**

after another, the obstacles keep turning your main character's world upside down, presenting greater challenges and more sacrifices.

Real obstacles have no obvious solution.

Discovering obstacles that present a dilemma can be difficult to imagine. When we've already seen the solution, the choice seems obvious. No matter whether it really happened or it's just taking place in our mind, we must forget the outcome and imagine how it was when the answer wasn't obvious at all.

If your character runs and doesn't stand up and fight, he'll lose all respect. When the relationships she treasures most will be lost, she faces an emotional death that will be a sword thrust through her heart. Either way, whether fleeing or fighting, your character will most certainly be facing some kind of death. There is no way out. Saying that is easy, but showing it in a way that readers will believe it's true will require considerable thought, writing, and rewriting to get the words right.

Your readers are smart enough to know that their hero must find a way out. They anticipate it. They expect it. And it's your job to make it impossible to see how your hero will survive. But when the unexpected happens and it makes perfect sense to them, they'll feel rewarded.

Formidable foes show the importance of the goal.

Obedience is words without emotion and meaning until obstacles put it to the test. Every change in desire and action needs a cause, which is revealed in the obstacles.

We need roadblocks to force detours, or our character has no reason to change direction. First comes the cause, then the evaluation and reaction. Which way will she go? When readers want to know, they'll keep turning the pages.

> **Difficult choices teach the best lessons.**

If your writing puts the effect before the cause, you're telling, not showing, explaining instead of letting what happens reveal the truth.

Let an expert tell her that her choice won't work, and readers will think it could. When two experts say it won't work, they're even more sure it could. How could the experts be wrong? That's for you to know and readers to find out.

Give your character an undefeatable foe, an impenetrable obstacle, and give him the means to win. And then what readers thought would work doesn't work, and you can move to the more-rewarding Plan C.

Best friends don't always agree.

Story is always about characters who want something but can't get it. Obstacles stand in their way, which most frequently should come from people, not places and things. Battling hurricane-force winds or surviving an earthquake might be dramatic, but another person who wants to go a different way makes the struggle personal. The unexpected betrayal of a friend is most significant.

Among Jesus' twelve disciples, who stands out as most significant? Certainly, the loyalty of those closest to him are important. Peter's impulsiveness stands out. James and John wanted to call fire down from above. Only one person of the remaining nine gave Jesus' sacrifice the most meaning—Judas, the betrayer.

- King David said it this way: *My trusted friend who ate bread with me has turned against me. We had heart-to-heart talks and together joined the throng of worshipers in God's house.* — Psalm 41:9; 55:14
- Job's great suffering was friends who turned against him: *My closest friends now hate me. Those whom I loved have turned against me.* — Job 19:19
- Our great hero, Peter, is best known for his betrayal: *Jesus turned and looked at him. Then Peter remembered what Jesus had said: "Before the rooster crows, you will deny me three times."* — Luke 22:61

Sticks and stones may break our bones, but the people we love are the ones who can hurt us the most.

> **Let readers sense danger that the character can't see.**

We have external and internal obstacles.

The struggle within ourselves is the most personal and real. The apostle Paul recognized the struggle within as a major battle. *"A battle rages between what we know in our hearts and what our minds and bodies say would be good. I don't do what my spirit says I should do, so I wind up doing what my moral instincts condemn"* (Romans 7:15).

If we want to captivate readers, we should introduce more and more tension from the internal struggles, not just add more dramatic events from another storm or person carrying a sword.

- Internal struggles are resolved when a question is answered about ourselves.

- External struggles seek to solve a problem by defeating an enemy, which could be a person, an ideology, an animal, the weather, or any other person, place, or thing that opposes your character's desire.

The greater the internal struggle, the more you will reveal the change in your character.

Dilemmas created by obstacles are the life of a story.

Obvious choices are the downfall of story. The lesser of two evils or the greater good is too easy. What would your character never consider doing? Now find the obstacle that would force him to think he must do what he would never do.

Nothing hooks readers more than your main character's crucial dilemma. It's not how nice she is or how bad he is that makes the difference. It's the problem, the challenge, the necessity that put equally strong convictions in opposition to each other.

> **Unseen obstacles can be life-threatening.**

You can't expect readers to remain engaged when your character makes a choice for no apparent reason. Give her a reason. That's good. Give her two equal and opposite reasons, and you have a wonderful dilemma that will keep readers up at night.

One obstacle is not enough.

Weak stories come from easy victories from a quest that faced few obstacles. Strong stories result from overcoming many obstacles of increasing severity that ultimately demand the highest sacrifice.

Your story needs turning points that aren't always easy. Without failures, complications, and setbacks, you will lose all but your most loyal readers. To hold the attention of a large audience, show them your character's desperation to have something of great value and increase the drama with more and bigger obstacles that demand the greatest sacrifice.

Plight

What good is it, fellow believers, if you think you
should write but fail to do the work? Can your
belief alone get your book written? — James 2:14

For your story to have significant value, you must consider the plight—how you will reveal the great consequence of your character's success or failure in reaching the objective. For each scene and chapter, keep asking your character, "What difference does this make? Why does it matter?" If what happens doesn't thrill or chill your character to great depth, readers won't be that concerned either.

Story is a quest for something of great value.

A story should have its disappointments and failures, but that is never the goal. There must be a great reward for success and a high cost for failure. The greater the sacrifice to avoid a tragic loss, the greater the reward and the more satisfied your readers will be.

The salvation message is cheapened by the idea that it's free—as if there is no plight. You don't have to do anything. While it's true that nothing can "buy" eternal life, we should know that it's far from free. What's the cost? Everything. Our lives. Remember, Jesus said we can't be his disciple without being willing to give up everything (Luke 14:33). When he said we must "take up our cross" in following him

> **Without something to lose, nothing will be gained.**

(Luke 14:27), he was talking about the necessity of losing our lives for the greater value of living with him forever.

If story is a quest for something of great value, then all stories are a kind of "salvation" message in which your character will experience transformation at great cost.

For your hero to save his life, he will have to put his life at risk, being willing to lose it.

Plight is a life or death matter.

Without an objective, readers don't know what a story is about. Without plight, what the character wants doesn't matter that much.

> Wherever life exists, death is a possibility.

A trip to the refrigerator is an unimportant event unless we understand his hunger. If it's 4:30 in the afternoon and he has eaten nothing all day, we know he's more serious than looking for a snack. Do readers care? Not much.

Put his life at risk. Then it matters. Maybe he's diabetic, on the verge of a coma if he doesn't reach the insulin in the refrigerator before he passes out. Now we have something serious enough for people to keep reading.

Death comes in many forms.

The threat of death poses the question whether there could be life after death. What will that life be like?

- Physical death offers pain for a moment, and then it's over.
- Professional death forces your character to find a new life.
- Psychological or emotional death can have major impact in your story, because the wounds may never quit hurting.

Imagine a teenager saying, "I'll just die if . . .

- nobody asks me to the prom."
- I can't play football."
- Janet dumps me."

58

- I don't get that scholarship."
- silly Willie gets valedictorian instead of me."
- I don't make the cheerleader squad."

Imagine an adult saying, "I'll just die if …

- I don't get that promotion."
- Francine says no to my marriage proposal."
- I can't go hunting with the boys."
- I have to declare bankruptcy."
- someone else is promoted to executive vice-president."
- the boss won't give me time off to see my sick mom."

None of these items might be regarded as all that important unless our storytelling shows how the character treasures it. Whenever readers see that the loss makes life no longer worth living, we have a life-or-death plight that will hold their attention.

The bark is better than the bite.

Death is easy. Life is over, and so is that part of the story. The fear of death can go on forever, so that is where we find the greatest plight.

Fear and tension escalate as we get closer to that life-or-death moment. Will she live or die? Keep the fear of death going for as long as you can.

Plight must be personal.

> Death means nothing without character involvement.

The sky is falling. The walls are closing in like a trash compactor. The bomb's clock is ticking. Big deal. Why does any of that matter?

We don't need more action. Another explosion. A wreck. Someone else is killed. We're immune to this stuff. We need the emotional attachment of a person who has a lot at stake. And then we need to see the struggle.

Chase scenes might be thrilling, but they won't bring us to tears unless readers care what happens to the characters in the story.

Story can be weakened as more and more things go wrong, but it is strengthened when something *worse* goes wrong. We want to intensify a struggle, not just add more problems.

Look for ways to increase the tension.

> The better things are, the more can go wrong.

Eliminating a negative can double the positive effect, so look for the tension killers and eliminate them. Sameness and predictability are great ways to disengage your reader. What might those areas be?

- Wording: Sameness in the wording, missing the variety that is the spice of life.
- Personalities: Characters are too much alike.
- Events: The same kinds of things are happening.
- Obstacles: The struggles are much the same.
- Objectives: Characters are working to accomplish the same things.
- Dialog: Characters talk like they are the same sex, age, culture, and belief.

With the negatives eliminated, your plight tools for increasing tension become stronger:

- Use the ticking time bomb.
- Bring the danger closer.
- Make the consequence worse.
- Remove possible solutions.
- Add a moral dilemma.

The greater the plight, the more that readers will be captivated by your story. Letting the tension wane will kill its forward momentum.

Insight & Transformation

Writers in the Kingdom of Heaven bring forth treasured stories that are familiar yet refreshingly new. — Matthew 13:52

The value of a scene, chapter, or book is shown by the important lesson learned that results in a change in the character. If the character learns nothing, then the reader learns nothing.

Change is the result of something important happening.

Your character has a goal. She wants something. The change is the unexpected result that you must be able to identify at the end, or you have no evidence to show that the scene has value.

She may not recognize any change, even at the end, but you should. If she exits the same as she entered, we have news, just telling what happened. We don't have story.

Something about the character must change.

> One thing changing is sure to change something else.

Plots have countless varieties.

Some have identified four main plots. Others think there are seven. But this is like asking, "How many slices does a pizza have?" It all depends on how you slice it.

In its greatest simplicity, a plot has a character fighting for and against something. A truth about life is revealed, and the experience brings a change in the character that otherwise wouldn't have happened.

Plots have value when readers experience the change that benefits the character.

Here are a few plot varieties:

- Rags to riches
- Coming of age
- Survival of the fittest
- Search for the treasure
- Defeat of the monster
- Leaving home
- Return to our roots
- Solving a problem
- Recovery from loss
- Answering a question
- Escape from oppression

The best plots not only change the character, but also the reader is changed by the experience of being the character in the story.

Character change is the driving force of story.

Since readers enjoy a happy ending, they expect your main character's struggles to somehow be resolved. Your hero's life will never be the same. Like the butterfly, his story will emerge from the escalating tension and tragedy to a soaring triumph of beauty.

Some writers say stories should be plot-driven. Others say they should be character-driven. Which should it be? Without a change in the character, neither approach works.

> **Nothing moves until something changes.**

People don't change until they are forced to change. With plot, we might identify the obstacles that will push our hero in a direction he otherwise would never go. Characterization could show your hero's objectives that give the story purpose. But the driving force must be the tension and conflict experienced by your characters in the pursuit of what they want.

Your story's success is measured in the transformation.

The most dramatic aspect of any story is the main character's growth and transformation. Every scene and chapter should advance the process of change at significant cost.

Without an enemy and a battle, there can be no victory. If the plight is missing, with few struggles and dilemmas, making the victory too easy and obvious, then the change isn't enough to be considered a transformation.

The difference between the caterpillar and butterfly needs to be remarkable and memorable. We want to see the transformation gradually through escalating challenges, so readers have to keep turning the pages to discover what will happen next.

Transformation must be shown, not told.

In a deep point of view, readers cannot be told the difference in your main character's thoughts and feelings. Actions, reactions, and dialog must show that the butterfly is no longer a caterpillar.

> **Transformation isn't real until it happens in the reader.**

When characters say what is on their minds, readers share their feelings, so they don't have to be told. Your description of expressions and actions should create such a vivid picture that any explanation would be redundant.

Don't linger too long in narrative summary that necessarily explains. When is narrative summary inappropriate? When your character wouldn't want to get into all the details. When you want to get to the next point of important action more quickly.

Unresolved Problem

Those who love God and keep writing their stories to fulfill his purpose should know that all their rejections will work together for good. — Romans 8:28

To keep readers turning the pages or want to buy the next book, we need to recognize the unresolved problem that points to the next great concern. Something always comes *next*.

But wait! There's more!

Readers are smart. They recognize overused literary devices like the obvious cliffhangers. Avoid those, because they damage the realism of the story. Instead, close your section breaks and chapters with conditions that will move the story forward.

> Fair weather shouldn't last very long.

Breaks between action sequences are like dips in a roller coaster ride bringing closure to what just happened, reorienting readers to what the main character wants and what is at stake, and preparing for a bigger thrill.

Never let your story come to a screeching halt at the end of a chapter.

Use the lull before the storm.

The congregation may drift off to sleep during a preacher's theological exposition, but everyone wakes up when he begins to tell a story. Why? Answer: *anticipation*. People expect to be encouraged, entertained, and enlightened.

Simply adding action is like the preacher jumping and shouting to make his message better. Focus less on the action and build anticipation with the recognition of an unresolved problem that says a storm is coming.

The end is just the beginning.

Life has its interludes—a night out for dinner, a Saturday at the beach, or a backyard barbeque—a time to relax and enjoy the moment. Without a time of reflection and orientation before what comes next, readers won't see your story as true-to-life human behavior.

> **The answer can't magically appear, but the next big problem can.**

In this time when your main character is catching his breath after something has gone wrong, he's finally feeling better, becoming energized. But for what is he energized? The next bad thing that is about to happen.

S C O O P I T U P

Putting SCOOP into Practice

"Writers are like the salt that makes food taste good," Jesus said. "But if the salt doesn't make the audience like the taste of the message, where is its value? You have a worst-selling book that will gather dust on the shelf or be thrown away." — Matthew 5:13

Instead of forcing your characters to conform to an outline, bring to life by identifying where they are, what they want, and where they're headed.

Make a simple SCOOP list.

For each scene and chapter, you just need to know the situation,

> Without practice, we can't get better.

who your main character, and the objective, obstacle, and plight. For the book and movie *The Ultimate Gift* by Jim Stovall, the SCOOP might look something like this:

- **S**ituation: A billionaire dies, leaving his wealth for a feeding frenzy among his heirs.
- **C**haracter: Jason Stevens, a favorite grandson.
- **O**bjective: His inheritance.
- **O**bstacle: Fulfill twelve conditions of the will.
- **P**light: Failure not only risks the money, it determines the value of relationships.

To strengthen the mental picture, write a two-sentence summary like this:

After a billionaire dies, leaving his wealth for a feeding frenzy among his heirs (Situation), favorite grandson Jason Stephens (Character) wants his inheritance (Objective). Can he fulfill the twelve conditions of the will, (Obstacle), or will he lose the money and valuable relationships as well (Plight)?

With just these five elements in a summary, you have the beginnings of great back-cover copy for your book. For a scene or chapter, you know you have the crucial aspects of story covered and can effectively describe the emotional journey of your characters.

Anticipate the outcome with SCOOP IT UP.

At the beginning, your character faces obstacles in getting what she wants. She doesn't know what will happen, what she will learn, or how she will change—but she will. Then she will face a new, unresolved problem.

In summary, you may anticipate the insight, transformation, and unresolved problem before you write the chapter. Or when you finish the chapter, you might learn what that is. Anticipation can give you a sense of direction as you write, but don't let your plan force your character. Let the character's thoughts, actions, and reactions occur naturally, and be

> **A starting point and direction are the most important parts of getting there.**

ready to adjust what turns out to be the appropriate change in character and the problem that needs to come next.

Suppose we wanted to write a scene about Herod's effort to find the baby Jesus. We want Herod to be the main character so readers will feel his cunning and passion to kill anything that might threaten his reign. What's the situation, the obstacles, and plight? By the end of the scene, what will he learn (insight) and how will he change (transformation)? What will come next (unresolved problem)?

A summary basis for guiding what you will write might look like this:

- S: After hearing news of a Jewish king's birth,
- C: Herod
- O: wants to squelch the rumors and kill the threat.
- O: If he can't intimidate the leading priests and teachers of the Law, and the people won't cooperate in finding the infant,
- P: will he lose his control over the Temple leadership and command of the people?
- I: Upon learning the location of the birth, Herod realizes that his only hope is to do what he has always done—send spies to identify the source of the rebellion.
- T: He cannot afford to be lenient and knows he must deal with the problem quickly and decisively,
- UP: but what will he do if the baby isn't found?

> **Practice makes the prize possible.**

You'll spend extra time writing summaries like this. Should you do one for every scene? Absolutely. You'll not only save time in the long run, but you'll also have a stronger scene, focused on what matters most to the main character.

The Writing Process

Let your writing shine so people may read your words
and glorify God in Heaven. — *Matthew 5:16*

An aspiring writer once told a literary agent, "Don't change any of my words. God gave them to me."

After a glance at the first page of the manuscript, the agent said, "I don't blame God for giving you these words. I wouldn't want them either."

When God's voice lives in the writer's words, stories are powerful, sharper than any two-edged sword, penetrating to the depths of the human soul, exposing thoughts and feelings. — *Hebrews 4:12 paraphrase*

A lot of work needs to be done before your God-given words are ready to share with the world.

Writing is hard work.

> Something worth writing is worth the cost of writing it well.

Some writers think seasoned authors can write a great novel in a month and it's ready for publication. That's not how the process works, not even for bestselling authors.

After six months of writing four hours almost every day, a great author might average no more than 750 words per day. That's just three double-spaced pages, about as many words in an hour as we can say in just one minute.

What takes so long? They write and rewrite, agonizing over gaps in the flow of events, weaknesses in believability, and tension that isn't strong enough. On a good day, they might write

69

2,500 words and at the same time delete 2,000 words of distractions, detours, and unnecessary details. They will reread, rewrite, and improve a scene before they begin the next one, knowing that this process will improve their focus on what needs to happen in the chapters that follow.

Because they are so good at their craft, they have to work and work and work until the manuscript is the best they know how to write.

When the work gets tough, the tough work harder and sacrifice more.

The one thing you can't afford to do is quit. Becoming an overnight success will often take twenty-five years or more.

When writers realize how hard it is to make bad writing good, good writing great, and great writing into something that captivates the world, they face two options. Two of them are bad—they can either quit or become content with where they are. The apostle Paul would tell us never to do that, no matter the cost.

> How people act and what they do means more than what they say.

Fellow writers, I've not yet become the best I can be, but I know one thing: I need to put past failures and successes behind me and focus on doing much better in the future. I must value the heavenly reward that comes from following Jesus Christ in using my God-given storytelling talent to the best of my ability. — *Philippians 4:13–14*

The third choice is where you want to be. Refuse to give up, and always strive to do better, no matter how small or great your writing success might be.

Hard work has inevitable rewards.

Conferences, seminars, and classes offer training that can make the path to success look simple and easy. Watching podcasts and reading how-to-write books can improve your skills, but the nitty-gritty work still has to be done. Is the benefit worth the time and effort? Absolutely.

The world measures success in dollars and numbers of copies sold, but that valuation is nothing compared to the benefit Christian writers receive for only one changed life. Readers will seldom say thank you, because they won't often recognize how your stories have changed their lives. But God knows, and that's what matters most.

Keep writing, always striving to do better, because the first life you change will be your own.

Pick up the sword.

> **With God on your side, quitting is the only way to lose.**

The worst story is the one never written. Jesus condemned the man who buried his talent (Matthew 25:25). The apostle Paul encouraged his disciples to stir up the gift within them (2 Timothy 1:6). You can't sharpen your skills until after you pick up your talent, begin to wield that sword, and keep practicing.

Quickly now, write that first draft so you can get to the sharpening stage.

Sharpen first, polish later.

Don't be a grammar freak. Forget about the proper writing style that we all learned in school—a style that would make your story as boring as everybody else's.

Use your natural voice to focus on the action and feeling in your story. Concentrate on your hero, how she fights through tough obstacles with the hope of achieving what matters most to her. Show us what she learns and how she changes from one chapter to the next.

After you have a really sharp story, then you can polish up the grammar, punctuation, and making better sentences.

A dull edge makes ineffective writing.

Constructive criticism feels like a contradiction of terms. How can anything that tears down be constructive? It happens whenever the benefit of the new exceeds the cost of what's torn down.

The sword must sustain significant pain when it's pushed against the grinding wheel. Flashes of splintering steel fly into the air. Likewise, you may wince when people's comments grate on your ego. Be thankful that someone took the time to say something. Most people don't. One reader's insight may not be right, but you can still use it as an incentive to find better words, something sharper, more effective.

> Sharpness always makes the cutting easier.

Sharpening happens one stroke at a time. With each rewrite and editing pass, a little roughness can be peeled away.

- Is your writing clear and concise?
- Do the events move rapidly forward in sequence of time and thought?
- Does the opening grab attention?
- Does the intensity of the challenges escalate the tension as the story progresses?
- Is the story believable? The truth will not be embraced by readers if it's not believable.
- Is there an important lesson learned?
- Does the character change from the experience?

Create a cutting edge.

With the first improvement, don't think the job is finished. Be honest with yourself and recognize the weaknesses in your story, even if you don't know how to fix them. Give your mind time to process that information—several days. Invariably, you'll think of something. Then just do it. Keep making it better.

A sword has a long edge. The entire edge needs to be sharp, not just an inch toward the center. Yes, one scene may be captivating, but what about the others?

Many great authors admit that they write terrible first drafts. But what makes them so good is their willingness to spend lots of time rewriting.

Only the right words will give your audience the right picture.

If you don't have a picture in mind when you write, your words can't be very good. If you want your words to be more captivating, go back and create more-vivid pictures in your mind. The better the picture—with situation, character, objective, obstacle, and plight—the better you can fill the blank page.

> For 1,000 readers, the same great words can create a 1,000 different pictures.

No matter how good a writer you are, you face an impossible goal—transfer your mental picture to the minds of your readers. Your only means to accomplish that are your words.

From your mental picture, you write the words. Perfect. Each day that follows, rereading those words will refresh the images you had before. Still perfect. But actually, they only *seem* perfect.

Have you ever set aside a story and didn't read it again until many weeks later, maybe months? When that happens, you may find yourself thinking, *What did I mean by that? This makes no sense. Why don't I have a good picture of what's happening?* Just about everybody has had that experience, even the best professionals. Why?

In the time away from your story, your mental picture was lost. When you read the story later, you became like your reader, having to create the images solely from your words. Therefore, as best you can when rereading a scene, try not to have a mental picture. Imagine being your reader, and create a new picture relying only on the words.

Readers need time to understand your story world.

If you're a planner and plotter, you know most of the story before you begin. You know all your characters, where they are, and where they're going. You're familiar with their history, what they like and dislike, and what they want. You know this very well for your hero and villain, but that's not all. You've named dozens of secondary characters and know them like rookies who have been riding with you for a while. But wait! Not so fast. Readers know none of this.

> **Readers need time to know your characters as well as you know them.**

In the first chapter, your main character is a total stranger to your readers. They will need several chapters to know enough to really care. Secondary characters quickly complicate readers' ability to remember who those characters are and why they matter. Be careful not to introduce too many characters too fast, which can confuse readers, and the tension and concern for what happens next will be lost.

Several days might pass before your reader picks up your book again and reads the next chapter. Will they remember Jack from two chapters ago and know he's a retired carpenter and your hero's uncle? Not if he's just one of several secondary characters, none of whom were given much attention in the story.

Never expect readers to know what you know—unless your words have made that information memorable.

Poetry

*Writing sprinkled with humor is wonderful medicine,
for pleasant words are like honeycomb, sweet to the
soul and healing to the bones. — Proverbs 16:24*

Poetry is a wonderful way to communicate thought and feeling.
With its structure, rhyme, and meter, you create a kind of music
that emphasizes your message. You motivate readers to laugh or
to cry.

Whatever you do, your lines must stir
emotion. The challenge of writing poetry
with rhyme and meter has been likened to
crafting a crossword puzzle using only words
that flow from the heart.

> Poetry speaks a
> second language
> of song.

The Beat of Little Feet

Readers tap their mental feet in rhythm in response to a pattern
of light and hard stresses. The beat is set in measures, called feet.
Adjacent syllables of the same stress must be separated by a space
or hyphen. An iambic pentameter has a light stress followed by a
heavy one, like this:

| I **thought** | you **said** | you **marched** | your **feet** | in **time** |

The Beat Continuing

Combinations of light and hard stresses define the type of meter.

1. Iamb (ī-am) is one light followed by one hard stress as in:
    | to **day** |.

2. Trochee (trō-kē) reverses the iamb sequence, hard followed by light: | **dai** ly |.

3. Anapest (an'-a-pest) uses two light stresses and a hard, forming a tripping sound that quickens the pace: | on my **way** |.

4. Dactyl (dak'-til) in repetitive use, creates a somewhat grotesque, incantation effect. It reverses the anapest sequence, a hard followed by two light stresses:
   | **march** ing in | **cess** ant ly | **rap** id ly |**press**ing on |.

5. Pyrrhic (pir'-ik), with two light stresses, often appears at the end of a line: | I **hear** | my **dear** | an **ech** | o ing |.

6. Spondee (spon'-dē) are two hard sounds that often follow a pyrrhic: | She **shed** | a **tear** | for a |**lov er** |.

7. Amphimacer (am-fim'-e-ser) contains hard/light/hard stress: | **cap** i **tal** |.

8. Amphibrach (am'-fe-brak) is the reverse of amphimacer, light/hard/light: | re **place** ment |.

Counting the Steps

Every sound group, such as iamb, anapest, or dactyl, counts as a *foot*. In music, we would count the *measures*. Line types are defined by the number of feet, beginning at two: dimeter, trimeter, tetrameter, pentameter, hexameter, heptameter, octometer.

> A poetic story can be more powerful than prose.

For the special skill and effort required, a great poet is recognized as a special kind of writer.

Free Verse

Some have said *free verse* is writing without pay, which may be the case more often than we would like. Seriously, the term refers to non-rhyming poetry with irregular cadence. *Structured free verse* is written to a preconceived format.

"The Web" by Frank Ball

Today, the fly buzzes in and out, up and down,

Moving with nonchalant ease,
Free to go wherever he pleases.
He darts back and forth
With no concern for his life,
Because he smartly avoids every threat.
His sharp, watchful eyes anticipate danger
And he quickly blasts off to the side.
Time after time he proves what he sees.
"I'm very good at escape," he says, "so they'll never catch me."

The Sonnet

In England, Shakespeare helped promote the sonnet, a fixed verse form of Italian origin, consisting of fourteen lines that are typically five-foot iambics rhyming according to a prescribed scheme. The common rhyming patterns are Shakespearean **abab cdcd efef gg**, Italian **abba abba cde cde**, and Spenserian **abab bcbc cdcd ee**.

> One great value of poetry is its consistent, measured beat.

The Villanelle

Next to the sonnet, the most common poem format, using two rhymes in five three-line and one four-line stanza, ending with two repeating lines. For example: **A1 b A2 a b A1 a b A2 a b A1 a b A2 a b A1 A2**, where the capitals indicate a repeated word and the letter values, a rhyme. A four or five-foot line works best, because shorter lengths call too much attention to the pattern.

The Sestina

Generally regarded as the most difficult form, made popular by French poets called *troubadours*. It uses only six ending words in six six-line stanzas, with three more lines at the end. Adding to the difficulty, in that three-line conclusion you must use the three unused words of the six somewhere else within the line.

Here's how the pattern looks, if we designate A-F as the ending words of the first stanza: **ABCDEF FAEBDC CFDABE**

ECBFAD DEACFB BDFECA concluded with **ECA** or **ACE** with **BDF** within the line. To be pleasant reading, the topic must be inherently repetitious.

The Pantoum

Composed of any number of four-verse stanzas in a repeating form 1234 2546 5768 . . . with the beginning lines one and three repeated in the concluding stanza's lines four and two. Meter or rhyme are not required.

> Poetry comes at higher cost per word and greater value than prose.

The Ballade

Three eight-line stanzas rhyming **ababbcbC** with a four-line conclusion **bcbC** where lines **C** repeat and rhymes with the ending word in line **c**.

The Triolet

Four two-line stanzas rhyming **AB aA ab AB** where capitals indicate repeating lines and the same letters rhyme.

Rondeau

A three-stanza, thirteen-line poem with a wrap-around rhyme in the form **aabba aabR aabR** where the beginning word or phrase is repeated at the end of the last two stanzas.

The Limerick

A five-line humorous poem in the form **aabba** where the first, second, and fifth lines have three stresses, and the third and fourth have two.

"Cracks in the Mirror," a four-stanza limerick by Frank Ball

> *Ignoring the cracks in the glass,*
> *He noticed a change from the past.*
> *Although he was old,*
> *He'd learned to be bold,*
> *And wear a big smile that would last.*

To bounce up and down on his knee,
His granddaughter shouted with glee.
She gave him a hug.
His arm held her snug,
And he was as glad as could be.

The Lord did create in his grace
What he could now see on his face.
Each day at the mirror,
His joy became clearer,
Each crack a delight to embrace.

The wrinkles he paused to inspect
Were not anything to reject.
Above his round chin
He wore such a grin
For these were love's after-effect.

Building Great Sentences

Writers who develop excellent skills in their work
will be admired by their peers and will earn the
respect of those they don't know. — Proverbs 22:29

A sentence is one or more words that complete a thought with a period at the end. Really. Nouns and verbs may be helpful. Sometimes not.

Focus on the message.

As soon as your words are noticed, your message is lost, so you want to avoid a literary style with fancy words and long sentences. Write like you talk. Then seek to improve both the way you talk and the way you write.

> The importance of the message makes the words matter.

A great sentence is whatever communicates most effectively. As a rule, informal English is best, because most people don't regard reading as a formal, dress-up activity. Most readers aren't inclined to use a dictionary.

Avoid purple prose.

The Roman poet Horace wrote, *Your opening shows great promise,* but then he complained about *flashy purple patches,* associating fancy words with the practice of sewing expensive patches on cheap garments to add richness. That effort had the opposite effect from what wearers intended, sending a clear message that they were *not* rich.

Similarly, richness of detail is important in your stories, but you want to avoid flowery phrases that call attention to the words instead of the message. Your words are best when they are essential to the scene and are easily understood. Make your readers so captivated by the action in the scene that they won't notice the words.

At the beginning of his novel *Paul Clifford*, Edward Bulwer-Lytton wrote: *It was a dark and stormy night; the rain fell in torrents— except at occasional intervals, when it was checked by a violent gust of wind which swept up the streets (for it is in London that our scene lies), rattling along the housetops, and fiercely agitating the scanty flame of the lamps that struggled against the darkness.* In 1830, that might have been good writing, but today it's used as a classic example of bad writing. Never begin a story with landscape and weather. Why? Readers care about characters, not conditions.

Focus on the audience.

Is your audience male or female, young or old? Christians might be inclined to say, "This book is great for everyone." Can a cute girl enjoy a story written for her grandfather? Can a grandfather enjoy a story written for a cute girl? Absolutely. But a book written equally for both audiences won't be that good for either one.

Your voice naturally shifts when your focus moves from a grandfather to the cute girl walking beside him. The danger in writing to everyone is effectively communicating with no one.

> **You are the one person who will not be your audience.**

If your mind tends to visualize a broad audience, find a picture of someone who represents the ideal person in your audience, the one who is most eager to hear what you have to say. Post it near your computer screen. By constantly visualizing your reader, you can break the comfortable habit of talking to yourself as you write.

Speak the language of your audience.

Outside the church environment, our Christianese language sounds like Chinese spoken to an Englishman. All cultures struggle with understanding language that is foreign to their everyday speech.

The buzz words that excite us as Christians can be confusing, even offensive, to those who don't understand. What does it mean to be "washed in the blood." Sounds like a horror story, doesn't it?

Our faith words are real to us, because they support our relationship with God. But what about outsiders? Our religious expressions are often not understood or are misunderstood, even by those who attend church. They can have different meanings for Christians from different backgrounds. If we really want to be understood by others, we should address their concerns using non-church language.

> For a message to be understood, it must be spoken in the audience's language.

In the Appendix, you will find a table of Christianese words that you might want to replace with something more meaningful to your audience. These words are not necessarily wrong. We just need to be careful, making sure our audience understands what we're saying. That's because we have many hypocrites and unbelievers in our churches, who *act* like they believe but are actually still searching.

Focus on the flow.

We read a page from left to right, from top to bottom, one word after another. Events unfold one moment followed by the next. Thoughts come in an ordered sequence, one idea, thought, or memory leading to whatever naturally comes next.

Your stories need to move forward in the same way, from left to right, top to bottom. References to the past, using the past-perfect "had" verb form, interrupt the forward movement of the story. Passive voice and state-of-being verbs with sit still, not moving forward, or they move in the opposite direction from the way we read, moving backward.

Flashbacks, reflections, and verbs may be necessary, but always be looking for alternatives that will move your story forward. Push for active verbs in which the subject of the sentence does something, rather than just existing or being the recipient of the action. You want to write, "Johnny climbed the giant oak," not, "The giant oak was climbed by Johnny."

Focus on variety.

Sameness is boring, so we need to avoid redundancy in thoughts, words, or grammatical structure. Short sentences speed the pace. Long sentences slow it down. A little of both is nice, and one-word sentences are allowed. Absolutely.

Longer sentences should form a chain of phrases and clauses that take the place of short, choppy sentences, taken in the natural order of thought and action.

> **Bored readers can't be patient very long.**

In grade school, we might write: *Jane got up early. Jane got dressed. Jane ate breakfast. Jane went to town. Jane bought new shoes.*

Instead of repeating Jane's name so many times, we might write: *Up early, Jane got dressed, ate breakfast, and went to town, where she bought new shoes.*

Captivate readers with essential details.

Suppose your hero rushes into his apartment to get dressed for a date. Since he doesn't care about the pictures on the wall, the beer cans on the coffee table, or the dirty dishes in the sink, those details shouldn't be mentioned. They detract from what the hero's goal is, at the moment. Instead, point out the hindrances to meeting his date on time: He can't find a clean shirt. His shoes aren't polished. The landlord consumes precious minutes, demanding payment of the rent. Not only do these details heighten reader concern for love that might be lost, they say a lot about the hero's personality.

By leaving out details that aren't essential, scenes are strengthened because more focus is placed upon the action and the outcome. Use concrete nouns and active verbs so readers see and feel the character's desires. Make them care about the character and be desperate to find out what happens. Give them reason along the way to, gasp, laugh, and cry.

Focus your descriptions in these areas:

- Action and dialog that reveal your hero's personality.
- Scene details that affect whether the hero can get what he wants.
- Something that raises a question that cries for an answer.
- Information that, if lacking, would keep the story from moving forward.

Give details that make explanations unnecessary.

Your descriptions should strive for action and dialog that allow readers to make their own decisions about the characters and speculation about the future. You might write, *John was angry*, but that explanation won't let readers experience the emotion and make their own judgments.

> **Let readers see what's going on, and they won't have to be told.**

Anger comes in countless forms, and nothing is gained for the reader by saying he was angry, very angry, or extremely angry. Do a good job of showing the anger, any explanation of the kind of anger and its intensity would be redundant.

You deprive readers of the *feeling* of anger by *saying* someone was angry. But if you write, *John slammed his fist on the table, spilling coffee all over his manuscript*, readers know exactly how John feels.

Sharp Detail and Vivid Color

The Lord says, "I know the great things I have in mind for your writing—plans for you to succeed, not fail—so anticipate the future with eager expectation." — Jeremiah 29:11

Printed text may be black-and-white, but your scenes need to come alive in vivid color and sharp detail.

Picture your character.

Look at the woman in the picture above. Where is she? What is she thinking, feeling, and doing?

If confused, she may look away, shrug, or hesitate. After she clears her throat, her speech will likely slow and become lower in pitch and volume. If nervous, she might bite her fingernails, keep brushing her hair with her fingers, or fake a smile.

> **If the words don't create the picture, readers can't see what the author sees.**

The table of "Expressions, Posture, and Actions" in the Appendix contains a wealth of ideas that might help you create a better picture of your character, but be careful not to describe too much.

For your point-of-view character, you can't describe what she can't see. You're limited to her thoughts, speech, and actions, with as little explanation as possible. Your observed characters can't be described beyond what she can see, hear, and interpret, but that's not all. You should not describe more than what interests her at that moment. Anything more will dull, not sharpen the picture.

85

Make descriptions precise.

Over-description obscures the picture rather than enhancing it. Consider these examples:

- Janet set her four-inch-thick black leather briefcase on her spotless, polished mahogany desk.
- Sam's eyes rested on the tall, thin blue-eyed woman wearing a white blouse, short black skirt, and red stiletto heels.
- Peter gave a quick sidelong glance through the ornate cut-outs in the tall wall covered with ivy to see the children on the merry-go-round in the city park.

If these people were a main character in one of your scenes, much of this information would be obvious to the character and therefore unimportant. For Janet, all that's important is what she does with her briefcase. Sam can't see his eyes resting. Can he see the color of her eyes? That's doubtful. And he probably doesn't care about the color of the woman's clothing. With Peter, readers can't distinguish the difference between a glance, a quick glance, and a sidelong glance. His observation has way too much detail to be taken in the short time of a glance. So here's what might be better:

> **Fuzzy words create fuzzy pictures.**

- Janet slammed her briefcase onto her desk.
- Sam stared at the long-legged woman in the short skirt and stiletto heels.
- Through the cutouts in the ivy-covered wall, Peter watched the children on the merry-go-round.

Do you see how fewer words can intensify focus on what really matters? By forcing your perspective into the view and desires of the main character and by limiting your observation, thoughts, and reactions to only your concerns at that moment, you make what matters to you matter to your readers.

Make descriptions realistic.

Writers may be tempted to use *different* descriptions when they should be looking for *better* descriptions—something more precise.

- Susan's head tilted to one side.
- Tim lowered his chin.
- She made her way to the stairs.
- The odor assaulted his nostrils.

Is this really the way people would naturally describe their own actions? What meaning can readers derive from a tilted head? Would Susan say that about herself? Would Tim say he lowered his chin? Is there a difference between "made her way" and simply going to the stairs?

Constantly strive for narrative from the main character's perspective, and not what an observer might write. Better visuals can be created using common words:

> Some classic phrases belong in the trash, not the text.

- Susan nodded toward the man on her right.
- Tim stared downward, his chin touching his chest.
- She ran to the stairs.
- The odor made him cover his nose.

Make descriptions relevant.

Posture and actions are more important than a detailed description of a person's eyes. Except in the closest, most intimate situations, the color of a person's eyes isn't noticed, so it should rarely show up in our writing.

- Her gray eyes puffy with tears, Patty pressed her red lips together in a tight, flat line.
- Tom's somber brown eyes opened wide and drooped in sadness at each corner.
- Catherine narrowed her tender blue eyes and pursed her lips.

The above examples must be for an observed character, because the main character has no means to see or need to describe his eye color. Scratch the eye color, and try to create a more vivid picture with fewer words.

- Her eyes puffy with tears, Patty pressed her lips together.
- Tom's eyes widened with sadness.
- Catherine looked down, and her lips puckered as someone about to cry.

Did readers need to be told that Patty's lips were red? If they were purple, the color would be important. If you leave out information that would be naturally assumed, the reader's mental picture sharpens.

Make questions obvious.

You don't want readers to reach the end of a statement and be surprised that the sentence was a question. If the beginning of the sentence looks like a question, they won't have to reread to get the correct meaning.

- The short Hispanic dude blocked traffic and wouldn't let anyone pass for an hour?
- I guess there's no use hoping the cops won't assume the worst?
- She didn't know anything about what happened last night?

> Do your best to keep a sentence from being misread.

The longer the sentence, the more likely that readers will be confused when they reach the question mark and realize that they missed the meaning. How might we revise the examples to make the question obvious from the beginning?

- Did the Hispanic dude block traffic so no one could pass for an hour?
- Is there no hope that the cops won't assume the worst?

- How could she not know anything about what happened last night?

Avoid different labels for the same thing.

Aiming to avoid redundancy, writers are sometimes tempted to use different labels for the same thing. Jack might be an executive, friend, brother, father, coach, or bird watcher. But calling him anything other than Jack or "he" can confuse readers as they wonder if "brother" or "coach" might be someone different.

Never use a thesaurus to avoid repeating the name for something. If you referred to the road, don't later call it a street. Remember, readers have only your words to visualize your picture.

> **Another word for the same thing can be confusing.**

Say it in fewer words.

When one word will do, never take two.

- Patrick made a conscious effort to look surprised.
- Janie rolled her gaze to the white clouds drifting lazily above the treetops.
- He put on a smile.

A hundred years ago, we admired writers for their fancy words and long sentences. Not anymore. Your readers want to get the picture in as few words as possible.

- Patrick tried to look surprised.
- Janie stared at the clouds drifting above the treetops.
- He smiled.

Give actions and body language clear meaning.

A glance is short. Staring takes awhile. A nanosecond can't be staring, and seeing who walks in doesn't need a long description. How does a voice drift? Would our character say his vision was "assaulted"?

- He stared at the monitor for a nanosecond before turning to see who had walked through the door at the far end of the large room.
- Her syrupy, sweet voice drifted across the phone line.
- The bright lights assaulted his vision.

Look for clarity, not a conflagration of esoteric gesticulations.

- After a nanosecond glance at the monitor, he turned to see who had walked through the door.
- Her voice on the phone line dripped with sweetness.
- Under the bright lights, he squinted and shaded his eyes.

Be sense-able.

Let all the senses—sight, hearing, touch, smell, and taste—cause your character's world to make sense to your readers. One of the best ways to create vivid pictures is to ask yourself, *What was it like?*

> We need all our senses to understand our world.

We might easily describe what we saw and what we heard, but we brighten the picture and intensify the color by asking, *What did it look like? What did it sound like?* Such questions search for how our character is affected by what is seen and heard.

To further expand your character's world, ask, *How did it feel? What did it smell like? How did it taste?*

Use comparisons and analogies.

While *like* may be the most overused and misused word in modern culture, comparisons are what we desperately need to bring life to a scene. When Jesus referred to Herod as a fox, a single word said a lot about the cunning king's nature.

For an imagined condition, you might use "as if." He looked as if ___. She felt as if ___. Another great comparison word is "than." The storm was bigger than ___. The girl was prettier than ___. The sky was darker than ___.

For a comparison to be effective, it must fit the context of the scene. Ask yourself, *If I'm the character describing this situation, what would I say?* So the child cried. What was it like? Saying the character was attentive, disappointed, or surprised is a judgment, but showing what it was like lets readers create the emotion within themselves.

The goal is not to be clever or cute. You want comparisons that perfectly fit the character at that moment.

- Charlie folded and tucked it away like a secret treasure map.
- These were grown men enjoying life like ten-year-olds playing at recess.
- Sir William bawled like a child who had lost his mother in the shopping mall.
- His expression was like someone whose full-house poker hand had been beaten by four aces.

How did it feel?

Feelings are difficult to describe, because they are internal, with limited physical evidence that can take paragraphs, even whole chapters, to describe. If your character felt awkward, insecure, or thrilled, deepen the feeling by showing what it was like.

> Readers want to feel what the character feels.

- Fly casting with my left hand felt as natural as writing with my toes.
- My classmates' snickering made me feel like I had come to school dressed only in my night-shirt and underwear.
- In the boardroom, Stanton felt like a kid on his first day at school, when he needed to find the restroom.
- An eagle soaring on the wind could not have been more thrilled.
- His fifth-grade classmates looked at him as if he had just gotten his driver's license.

How did it look?

Smiles, smirks, and grins don't say much about the feeling behind the expression. A smile can be from humor, pleasure, or to conceal pain. Smirks aren't always condescending. And a grin is just another word for a smile.

For readers to see the scene clearly, show what it looked like.

- Papa grinned like a carnival game host watching a kid throw darts and miss the balloons.
- He looked as tough as a scuffed boot.
- The kids took their seats, assigned in alphabetical order like chess pieces, obliged to occupy a particular square before the game could begin.
- I smiled like a kid who was sure he could race cars after the first driving lesson.

How did it smell or sound?

> **The right words can add color to a black-and-white page.**

Tell readers that the odor was bad, the preacher's message was boring, or the tires squealed, and you have a simple picture. Add color by showing what it was like.

- Flying gravel pelted the bottom of the car, sounding like we were driving through a hail storm.
- I waited for Mom to say something, but all I heard was my sniffling and the clump-clump of the tires rolling across the brick road.
- I stepped over a shirtless, bearded man whose odor was strong enough to embarrass a skunk.
- Gasping, snorting, and chewing, Papa sounded like he had swallowed a foghorn with a broken reed.
- The preacher's words sounded to me like a recitation of the Declaration of Independence.

How did it taste?

Taste brings back memories quicker than any of the other senses. Describing what a situation tasted like can make readers' mouths water—or make them wish for mouthwash.

- The eggs tasted like Uncle Albert's cigarettes smelled.
- I loved beans, but this was about as tasteful as boiled cardboard.
- As the hamburger juice dripped down my chin, I enjoyed my chocolate malt, but kicking Jack in the teeth tasted better.
- As we caravanned through the city, I smelled burning garbage, raw sewage, and diesel smoke. I licked my lips, and the foul taste told me I should be content with dry lips.
- Charlotte was as sweet as Grandma's banana pudding.

Avoid indefinite qualifiers.

If Timmy was *very* small, how small was he? Exactly how long was the *long* rope, ten feet, twenty-five, or fifty? We need a comparison to see how tall a *tall* man really is. A *big* bear is just a bear until readers see it towering six feet above the Indian who holds a spear that feels like a toothpick.

> An approximation is only partly clear.

- The living room was very small.
- The storm was really big.
- Fred was exceptionally strong.

Give readers a vivid picture so they don't have to figure out how big, tall, long something is.

- The living room was as small as the bedroom she had as a child.
- The storm covered half of Texas.
- Fred could lift the rear of a pickup a foot off the ground.

Describe possible, imagined, or likely conditions as actions.

When readers are led to think abstractly, they are distanced from the present action. You don't want them running down a theoretical rabbit trail, getting lost from the story's live drama.

> Conditions aren't actions that can be seen and felt.

The verbs *could*, *would*, and *should* are abstract, referring to something that might exist, should exist, or probably exists.

When that is the only verb that works, use it, but only after trying the active expression.

- A relaxing evening *could* turn into an all-night prayer vigil.
- We *would* submit to the tests, only to find everything normal.
- Jonesy *could* hear the train coming.
- Billy *was able to* study hard and pass the test.
- Each morning, he *would* walk around the park.

People don't like blurred photos. You want to fill your world with clear, sharp pictures, not something fuzzy, weakly defined. A likely or possible action is not as engaging as a "real" action.

How might we improve the above examples?

- The relaxing evening turned into an all-night prayer vigil.
- We submitted to the tests, and everything was normal.
- Jonesy heard the train coming.
- Billy studied hard and passed the test.
- Each morning, he walked around the park.

Avoid approximations.

Attempting to be accurate, writers sometimes use expressions like, "Jason was around six feet tall." Really? Exactly how tall is *around* six? The problem is not the truth of the statement but that readers are left guessing. Let's see, he might be 5'10". That's close to six, isn't it? No, maybe he's taller. Could he be 6'3"? Leave out *around* and say he was six feet tall. Readers won't send you a nasty email if they find out he was only 5-11½.

- Their house was about a mile down the road.
- A crowd of 300 to 400 protesters gathered outside the courthouse.
- A few weeks ago, Jack decided to look for a new employer.

Your best guess is better than leaving readers to guess. Why? A specific number gives readers an immediate picture.

- Their house was a mile down the road.
- A crowd of 350 protesters gathered outside the courthouse.
- Three weeks ago, Jack decided to look for a new employer.

Saying *might* or *seemed* leaves readers to decide what's true, a condition sometimes appropriate and sometimes inappropriate for your point-of-view character.

- Suzanne seemed unable to look at the facts and make a rational decision.

If your main character is unsure about Suzanne, a question would be showing instead of telling.

- Could Suzanne look at the facts and make a rational decision?

People can be quick to make judgments, even if they are wrong. In that case, your main character sees "what is," not "what seems."

- Suzanne couldn't look at the facts and make a rational decision.

Absolutes can go too far.

Swearing something is true will put the

> Swearing the truth weakens every fact that isn't sworn.

truth into question. You might use *always*, *absolutely*, or *totally* to show passion for your viewpoint. What's wrong with that? If your audience agrees, the word isn't needed. If your audience thinks of an exception, your audience disagrees, and you risk losing them.

Jesus said we should just let our yes be yes and our no be no (Matthew 5:37). If we have to swear something is true, using *always*, then we leave readers to wonder about statements that don't use *always*. Are they even true?

Maybe it would be a good idea to always leave out *always*. No, it would be better to say: Maybe it would be a good idea to leave out *always*. Then, if you *absolutely* must leave it in, you can. No, better yet: If you must leave it in, you can.

Show Emotion

Explaining emotion with labels such as *angry, joyful,* or *frustrated* replaces the feeling with an observation. It's the difference between *being* angry and knowing *someone else* is angry. Readers want to experience the emotion, not be told about it.

> Readers must see it to feel it.

Lazy writers will tell readers that Billy is mad. If he wasn't just a little bit upset, they try to intensify the emotion by saying Billy is *really* mad, *very* mad, *terribly* mad, or *extremely* mad. Those qualifiers are little help in engaging readers.

Skilled writers take extra time and effort to visualize Billy. How is he acting? What is he doing? Is he yelling? Lying on the floor, kicking his feet and screaming? Describe his actions, expressions, and voice to create the emotional feeling that needs no explanation.

- Jack was worried.
- Suzanne was scared.
- John was excited.

These are passive, telling statements. To show the emotion, readers must see the physical conditions in action.

> *For five minutes, Jack paced back and forth, occasionally stopping to stare out the window. "No matter what I do, I'm in trouble." Back at his desk, he picked up the phone, keyed three digits, and stopped.*

Is Jack worried, scared, or excited? Definitely not excited. We have a feeling of worry and fear that builds tension.

Showing the emotion is worth the extra effort, because readers will keep turning the pages to find out what happens next.

Dealing with Dialog

*By the power of the Holy Spirit, we are skilled communicators of
the righteous work that only God can do.* — Psalm 71:16

Except for direct quotes in nonfiction, dialog should *represent* the
important parts of your characters' speech.

In real life, we often say too much or not enough. We use
clichés and meaningless words such as *like, you know,* and *so*. We
ramble and often repeat ourselves. We can talk endlessly about
trivialities—small talk that has nothing
to do with our goals and what bothers
us most.

> Balance between
> narrative and dialog
> makes the story real.

Make dialog relevant.

Effective storytelling calls for lines that build tension, voice the
worries and desires of your characters, and reveal more about
their personalities—who they really are. As the chapters unfold
and the characters change, we should see differences in their
dialog that reflect their new nature and goals.

If the dialog isn't essential to set the tone of the situation,
reveal more about the character, or advance the plot, leave it out
and focus on what matters.

Indirect dialog says more with fewer words.

In direct dialog, readers hear what characters are saying, with
quotation marks around the spoken words.

- "Hurry up, Johnny. The bus will be here in ten minutes."

Indirect dialog uses the narrator's voice, without quotation marks, to summarize what might be an hour of conversation.

- Mom said Johnny would miss the bus if he didn't hurry.

Both direct dialog and narrative description are good, but too much of a good thing is bad. Don't let your story be told mostly with dialog or mostly with description. Use a mix of dialog to make the story real and description to move it rapidly forward.

Said is the best tag verb.

When we refer to a "tag," we're talking about the "he said" or "she said" dependent clauses that identify the speaker—like a name tag. We don't want readers to stare at the tag, so anything more than *said* hinders rather than helps the dialog.

Some writers think *said* can be overused in a manuscript, so they use redundant substitutes like *continued, added,* and *proposed*.

> **Said can be said as many times as *said* needs to be said.**

That practice may be literarily acceptable, but it's not the best storytelling. We want a tag verb that *vocalizes* the speech, not *describes* it. In a proposal, we *say* the words, we don't *propose* them.

Understand that *said* is what we call an "invisible" word, like the articles *a, an,* and *the*. Nobody will complain about using *the* too many times in a chapter. In the same way, readers don't notice *said* in a sentence. It's as invisible as a grain of sand on the seashore.

We do *whisper* or *shout* words, but use them sparingly. We don't *exclaim* words, so *she exclaimed* doesn't work.

Since mumbling isn't intelligible speech, we don't want *he mumbled*.

Use body language, tone of voice, or action to identify the speaker.

Some writers are so passionate against using *said* tags that they always use standalone sentences describing something about the speaker. That's a good idea when the description adds meaning to the dialog, but if not, a *said* tag is better.

In a video of a couple sitting in a restaurant, arguing, the words might contain half the meaning, with the actions, body language, and tone of voice telling the rest of the story. Shouldn't that make tags unnecessary? Yes, as long as the descriptions are about the argument and not the meal.

Consider this example that uses no tags:

> *Patty stirred sugar and cream into her coffee. "Why do you let your boss walk over you like that?"*
>
> *"I don't want to lose my job." Bill took a bite of his steak.*
>
> *"You're such a weakling." Patty sipped her coffee. "Find another job."*
>
> *"Where?" Bill tried the green beans. "We can't afford a cut in pay."*

Can you see how the descriptions weaken the dialog? To fix that, we must revisit the scene and see how the character's tone of voice, posture, or action might add meaning to the dialog.

> Narrative and dialog should be as closely linked as bread and butter.

> *Patty glared at her husband, ignoring the food on her plate. "Why do you let your boss walk over you like that?"*
>
> *"I don't want to lose my job." Bill sounded like someone defending himself in court.*
>
> *"You're such a weakling." Patty leaned forward like a prosecuting attorney. "Find another job."*
>
> *"Where?" Bill squirmed, picked up his knife, and attacked his steak. "We can't afford a cut in pay."*

What gives an argument more meaning, how people are eating in a restaurant or court proceedings? Find the metaphor that strengthens the dialog, and avoid descriptions that don't matter.

Be sure the meaning of a related action is clear.

Nod means *yes*, and a shaking head means *no*, but other actions aren't that clear. In the Appendix under "Expressions, Posture, and Actions," you will see where a furrowed brow can indicate anger, anxiety, concentration, dread, fear, hatred, or sadness. Which is it? To make the meaning clear, you may need a metaphor to show what that action says.

What does a *tilted head* indicate? According to the Appendix chart, it might be listening, a sexual interest, or a sign of trust. Or it might be neck strain. Be sure the action has meaning so it will strengthen the dialog instead of weaken it.

- Dr. Kuptra furrowed his brow in a concerned look.
- Trina tilted her head with a desire to hear more.

Actions speak louder than words.

Since most expressions are involuntary, how your characters look can be as important as what they say. Don't miss the opportunity to identify the speaker with the action, body language, or tone of voice that reveals more than what the words can say.

> Both dialog and narrative are good, but too much of a good thing is bad.

Do people always say what they mean? Of course not. You have interesting characters when they say one thing but look and act like they mean something else.

- "That's okay. It doesn't matter." William walked out and slammed the door behind him.
- "I love you so much." Sarah glanced away, unable to look him in the eye.

Identify the speaker early in the dialog.

Some writers have a natural tendency to identify the speaker after the dialog. For lengthy dialog, that practice isn't good. Consider this example:

> *That sounds like a good idea. I know a lot of people who agree. In fact, I know a lot of people who agree. I have a business friend who would probably finance the venture." John sounded as confident as sunshine on a hot summer day.*

What's wrong with that? Readers have to listen to almost thirty words without knowing who is speaking. When the speaker identification comes at the end, the author is saying, "Remember that dialog you just heard, and now go back and put the right face with the voice."

You want variety, so avoid always putting the identifier at the beginning. But try to put it *near* the beginning, with a tag after an introductory phrase or the identifying sentence after the first piece of standalone dialog.

> *"That sounds like a good idea." John sounded as confident as sunshine on a hot summer day. "In fact, I know a lot of people who agree. I have a business friend who would probably finance the venture."*

Punctuation

*Without guidance, writers will fail, so blessed are those who
carefully follow publishing guidelines.* — *Proverbs 30:18*

When the referee blows the whistle, we have no choice but to
stop and worry about the rules. Ignore the rules, if you like. Don't
let them slow your rapid flow of words. Just write, and do it
quickly.

> Punctuation is one
> essential way to
> make a point.

But it's really nice to know the rules so
your natural writing doesn't throw so many
yellow flags when it's time to refine your
manuscript.

The punctuation officials don't always agree.

What one stylebook says is wrong might be preferred in another.
Different publishers can follow their own rules. If you're a self-
published author, you can write and punctuate however you want.

Guidelines, rules, and exceptions fill hundreds of pages of fine
print. No proofer can remember all the nuances all the time.
Computer programs that check spelling and grammar might flag
something that our eyes didn't catch, but they aren't always right.

What you see in print, even in traditionally published
bestselling books, will contain ambiguous words, confusing
phrases, and punctuation errors. Why? Perfection is an impossible
dream.

Strive for what is most important—captivating words that are
quickly understood by your readers. To do that, we do well to be
aware of the principles behind the punctuation rules.

102

Apostrophe

Sow your seeds in the morning and keep writing until dark,
for then you may reap a great harvest. Ecclesiastes 11:6

Apostrophes are used for contractions and possessive nouns, a simple task that is often misunderstood.

Know how to be possessive.

Most words form singular possessives by adding apostrophe-s. The biggest exception to that practice is with the name Jesus, because most people don't pronounce "geezusses" for the possessive form. Other names ending with *s* should usually be made possessive with an apostrophe-s. But if that doesn't sound right, you might want the punctuations to phonetically match your speech.

- Jesus' words deserve thoughtful consideration.
- Chris's new restaurant serves great steaks.
- The actress's part was short. (One actress had only a few lines.)
- Jack and Jill's house was listed for sale. (Jack and Jill share ownership of the same house, so apostrophe-s is added to "Jack and Jill."
- Jack's and Jill's houses were listed for sale. (Jack's house and Jill's house were both offered at the same time, so the apostrophe-s is added to both names.)

Plural words from their possessives by adding apostrophe-s. But if the plural ends with an s, only the apostrophe is added.

- The men's ballgame was rained out.
- The actresses' part was short. (More than one actress took part in one short scene.)
- The soldier had two weeks' leave.

Pronouns don't have an apostrophe.

Don't confuse the contraction *it's* (it is) with the possessive pronoun *its* that has no apostrophe. None of the possessive pronouns (his, hers, its, their, theirs, ours, yours, whose) have an apostrophe.

- Do you have its location?
- Do you know where it's located?

Words are never made plural with apostrophe-s.

The one exception is single letters and numbers.

- Does Billy already know his ABCs?
- Susie is five months old.
- Don had seven A's and two B's on his report card.
- John remembers what life was like in the 1940s.
- Katherine has a large collection of DVDs.
- The Jacksons live next door.
- There are no ifs, ands, or buts.

Use an apostrophe to form contractions.

Some writers think proper English should never use contractions, but they're important when that's the way we talk. In ancient English, possessive nouns didn't exist. The possessive pronoun was used. For example, if the book belonged to John, people would say, "A neighbor borrowed John his book." As the language evolved, "John his book" became "John's book."

An apostrophe is used to combine the meaning of two words into a single word that matches the way we talk.

- Don't you want to go? (Few native-born Americans would say, "Do not you want to go?")
- I know you're right. (Don't use the pronoun *your* when "you are" is meant.)

Use an apostrophe when letters are left out.

When the apostrophe is the first character, word processors want to turn the curl backward like a single-quote mark. Try holding down the Ctrl key and pressing the apostrophe twice. On some keyboards, you can hold down the Alt key and type 0146. Or you can type the apostrophe twice and delete the one that faces the wrong way.

- Caleb can't go 'cause he's got somethin' to do.

Colon

*Come and listen, all who respect God, and I will tell my
stories about what he has done for me. — Psalm 66:16*

Don't be confused by the period that has doorknob above it. The
dot at mid-level indicates a need to stop before readers open a
new area of related information.

Think of the open door.

Like the period, the colon requires a full stop, ending a complete
sentence before opening the door to an explanatory sentence or a
list of items.

- The speaker offered an important insight: "When we're in
  the valley," he said, "we should look up, for all deep valleys
  are surrounded by mountain peaks."
- Writing has three important elements: editing, revising, and
  rewriting.

It can be used in a book title to point to the subtitle, Bible
chapters to point to a particular passage, or to introduce a section
of text.

- *Eyewitness: The Life of Christ Told in One Story*
- Matthew 5:13
- To whom it may concern:

Unlike periods and commas, which always go *inside*, the colon
always goes *outside* the quotation marks.

- Here's what I put at the top of my "to-do list": wake up, brew a cup, and write.

Comma

Write for your children so they can tell their children, so your stories may live from generation to generation. — Joel 1:3

A comma functions like a yield sign, a pause to keep readers from having a train wreck with words crashing into the words that follow. A misplaced comma has been known to cost companies millions of dollars.

It is the most used and misused tool in the punctuation world.

Join sentences with a comma before the conjunction.

When you have two clauses that would stand alone as separate sentences, each with its subject and verb, we need both the comma and the conjunction to join them.

- John walked to town. He took a ride home.
- John walked to town, and he took a ride home.

When the two verbs share the same subject, we do not have a comma before the conjunction.

- John walked to town and took a ride home.

Pause after an introductory word or phrase.

For short openers, you might not want to pause. But most of the time, sentences will read better if you do.

- For one thing, we need to study the situation.
- If you'll turn the light on, we won't have to work in the dark.

Separate a question from a statement.

A natural pause keeps the statement from running into the question.

- Bill is coming, isn't he?
- I can't believe that, can you?

Separate a list of three or more items.

The *Associated Press Stylebook*, which is often followed for articles, approves no comma before the conjunction that concludes a list of items. That practice allows the last two items to be viewed as a single unit.

For example:

The shepherds found Joseph, Mary and Jesus lying in a manger.

Was Mary lying in the manger? Surely not. For clarity, the best approach uses the comma after all the items.

The shepherds found Joseph, Mary, and Jesus lying in a manger.

- Johnny found the bread, peanut butter, and jelly in the pantry.
- A soldier's favorite colors should be red, white, and blue.

Use a comma in place of *and* between two adjectives.

When two adjectives modify a noun, a comma isn't always needed. Sometimes it is. What's the difference? As a test, put *and* between the adjectives. If that sounds right, use a comma instead of the conjunction. Otherwise, you don't need a comma.

- John is a kind, intelligent young man.
- He stared vacantly into the clear blue sky.

Use commas to join dependent tags to dialog.

Since a tag like *she said* can't stand alone as a separate sentence, we need a comma, not a period, to link the clause to the dialog.

- "I've got a secret," Sammie whispered.

- "We should go," he said, "before the storm arrives."
- Mom said, "Johnny, you need to clean your room."

Laughing is an independent action that belongs in a standalone sentence. When the sentence works independent from the dialog, we want a period, not a comma.

- Patty laughed. "She looks ridiculous in that plaid dress."

Commas can be used to emphasize an adverb.

In the following examples with and without commas, notice the difference in meaning.

- We waited, patiently, for our son to get home.
- We waited patiently for our son to get home.

Commas separate explanatory but not restrictive phrases.

A phrase that restricts the meaning of what it refers to should not be separated with a comma. If the meaning doesn't change when the phrase is left out, then we need the comma.

- Peter, who graduates this year, plans to join the army.
- A man who wishes he had a friend isn't very friendly.

An interrupting word or phrase needs to be set off with commas.

The same rule applies when someone is addressed directly by name or title.

- I believe, no matter what the weather is like, we'll have a good time.
- When I'm writing, honestly, I'm in another world. (Without the commas, readers have to wonder what it's like to write dishonestly.)
- Listen, Jack, you don't have a job if you can't get here on time.
- That, sir, is the whole story.

Commas set off the year when it follows the month and day.

Without the day, no commas are needed to set off the year.

- On August 11, 1984, President Ronald Reagan joked about bombing Russia.
- Garry Kasparov faced IBM's chess-playing computer in February 1996 and won.

Commas set off degrees or titles that follow names.

Jr and *Sr* are now considered part of a person's name, so commas and periods are no longer required.

- William Henry, M.D., did the surgery.
- Jack Moncrief Jr built a financial empire.

Commas go *inside* quotation marks.

Unlike colons and semicolons, which always go *outside*, the comma always goes *inside* the quotation marks.

- After so many days reading "How to Write," I just needed to write.

Dash

I write honestly from my heart, seeking
to make the truth known. — *Job 33:3*

Dashes are joining characters of two different lengths, long and short, which serve different purposes. Both are longer than the hyphen.

The *n* is shorter than the *m*.

The en dash is about the length of an *n* and a little longer than a hyphen. Unfortunately, it can't be found on the keyboard. It's one of many special characters you can get through the *Insert > Special Characters* menu. Some keyboards produce it by holding down the Alt key and typing 0150 on the numeric keypad. Word processing's Autocorrect will sometimes produce it by typing *space-hyphen-space* between characters, but then you'll have to delete the spaces. Once created, another possibility is saving the character for copy and paste.

Use it for a span of numbers or dates.

- John 11:1–54 tells about Lazarus raised from the dead.
- Orson Welles (1915–1985) wrote *War of the Worlds*.
- Texas has its hottest weather in July–August.

The *m* represents the long dash.

The em dash is about the length of an *m* and twice the length of a hyphen. You can get it through the *Insert > Special Characters* menu. Some keyboards produce it by holding down the Alt key and typing 0151 on the numeric keypad. Word processing's Autocorrect will sometimes produce it by typing *hyphen-hyphen* between characters. Once created, another possibility is saving the character for copy and paste.

Use the em dash to end interrupted speech.

Correctly configuring the dialog can be tricky, because Microsoft Word doesn't know which way to curl the quotation mark after the em dash. One approach that usually works is to type the last word followed by two hyphens and two quotation marks. Word will autocorrect the two hyphens to an em dash, and you'll need to delete the quotation mark that curls the wrong way.

- "I want you to know I have—" Alex fell back, reeling from his wife's slap across his cheek.
- Sally said, "If you weren't so quick to pass judgm—" "But I'm not judging," Bill said.

A shift in thought can be interrupted speech.

- "I'm thinking about—John, are you paying attention?"

Dialog split with a concurrent action uses an em dash inside the quotation marks.

- "I believe I will find it"—he opened the drawer—"right here."

Use the em dash for long pauses.

Commas are preferred for most pauses, but sometimes you want a longer pause. The em dash can answer that need.

- With intricate detail, I described the Marauder J4—both its beauty and its importance.

Ellipsis

For God so loved the world that he gave his only son, so writers
who believe in him and share their stories will not die but will
lead others to eternal life. — John 3:16

An ellipsis is used to indicate trailing speech or left-out words.

Many editors don't like the three-dot type character and prefer typesetting three periods with non-breaking spaces in-between. You can create that configuration by typing a *period Ctrl-Shift-space period Ctrl-Shift-space* on a PC keyboard. Or you can get the non-breaking spaces through the *Insert > Special Characters* menu. Once created, you can copy and paste where needed.

Give your character pause.

Your hero hesitates, not sure what to say. A woman is distracted and turns her attention elsewhere. Fading speech may be indicated with an ellipsis, but if you want more, describe actions or expressions that explain the pauses in the dialogue. Pauses can be fun. Short delays can raise the tension. But don't overdo them.

Remember, your readers want to keep moving.

- "I don't know what to . . . I know, I'll do nothing."
- "Oh! How could . . . Um . . . Well I . . ." Jane smiled like a child on Christmas morning. "Thank you . . . Thank you very much."

Focus on a crucial point by leaving out words.

By leaving out words in a quotation, you add focus on what is left. Be careful though. You're not allowed to change the meaning of what someone has said.

Compared to Edward Everett's two-hour oration, Abraham Lincoln's 250-word address at Gettysburg was a lightning flash, short and loud. With ellipses, you can focus on the most important elements.

> *Four score and seven years ago our fathers brought forth . . . a new nation . . . dedicated to the proposition that all men are created equal. Now we are engaged in a great civil war, testing whether that nation . . . can long endure. We are met on a great battle-field of that war. We have come to dedicate . . . a final resting place for those who here gave their lives that that nation might live. . . . The world will little note, nor long remember what we say here, but it can never forget what they did here. It is for us the living . . . to be dedicated here to the unfinished work which they who fought here have thus far so nobly advanced. . . . that this nation, under God, shall have a new birth of freedom—and that government of the people, by the people, for the people, shall not perish from the earth.*

Exclamation Mark

*For you will tell your story to everyone—all
you have seen and heard.* — *Acts 22:15*

An exclamation is a shouting stop, used at the end of an emphatic command or interjection. The mark is often overused, signifying lazy or novice writing.

Emphasis comes from words, not punctuation.

If the words carry the emphasis, the punctuation isn't needed. If the words don't carry the emphasis, the punctuation doesn't help. Adding exclamation marks is like turning up the volume to make a message more impactful. It just doesn't work.

An absolute no-no is use of more than one exclamation mark.

As a general rule, use periods, not an exclamation mark. If that bothers you, then find ways to improve the words and resist the temptation to turn up the volume.

The one exception to that rule is single-word exclamations. We often need those when they seem appropriate.

- "No!" Juliet threw her half-full wine glass, shattering it against the restaurant wall. "I want a divorce."
- "Wow," Eeyore said. "I'm so-o-o happy." (The pessimistic donkey in *Winnie the Pooh* would never be excited about anything, not even in a single word.)
- "Johnny," Mom yelled, "I meant, do it now." (With the verb yelled, using an exclamation mark after Johnny would be redundant.)

Hyphen

So what can you say about your writing efforts? If God is on your side, you cannot fail. — Romans 8:31

Hyphens create compound words and break words into syllables. Unlike the dashes, which push items apart, the hyphen joins items to function as a single unit.

Join an adjective that modifies an adjective.

Two adjectives can independently modify a noun, but for an adjective to modify an adjective, a hyphen is needed for clarity. For word groups to function as a single-word modifier, they need to be joined with hyphens.

- The orange-juice buyer negotiated a lower price. (Without the hyphen, the juice buyer can be regarded as orange.)
- The city council approved the public-housing project. (Without the hyphen, the city approved a housing project that was open to the public.)
- A shepherd will leave the ninety-nine sheep to save the one that is lost. (Numbers and fractions, such as three-fourths, get a hyphen.)
- How do we make the choice when there are almost-equal alternatives?

Use hyphens to join compound modifiers.

- Four-year-old Johnny could recite the alphabet forward and backward.

117

- Patrick was a throw-caution-to-the-wind entrepreneur.
- William preached a fire-and-brimstone message last Sunday.

When successive compound modifiers share the same ending word, the ending word may be dropped, but keep the hyphen.

- The company uses both full- and part-time employees.
- The Happy Hippos class is for three- and four-year-old children.

Beware computer-generated hyphens.

For manuscripts submitted to editors and agents, don't justify the margins and don't hyphenate.

In preparing print-ready copy for self-publishing, you might consider not justifying the right margin and not hyphenating words at the end of a line. Many people find reading easier when the spacing between words doesn't widen to make the right margin even.

If you choose to automatically hyphenate, carefully proof the line endings for anything that might be misleading.

For example: *Re-pair* wrapped around so *re-* is as the end of a line and *pair* on the next line, could be misunderstood as "pair again." *Re-sign* could be taken to mean "sign for a second time."

Parentheses

Blessed are writers who receive many rejections, whose messages were good but didn't fit the publisher's needs, for the Kingdom of Heaven belongs to them. — Matthew 5:10

Parentheses can be like timeouts, interruptions that steal focus from the action of the game. Sometimes they are important, but they often need to be avoided.

Parentheses have limited value in nonfiction.

Parentheses have their greatest value in nonfiction writing when the main information needs to be supplemented with an off-the-road clarification or comment.

- Without saying anything, Earl slipped out of the house and boarded a flight to Moline (an Illinois city on the Mississippi River, his childhood home).

If the information is so much aside from the narrative that it needs parentheses, you might consider deleting it. Or you might make it part of the narrative without the parentheses.

- Without saying anything, Earl slipped out of the house and boarded a flight to Moline, an Illinois city on the Mississippi River, his childhood home.

Acronyms can be used instead of long names after they have first been defined in parentheses after the name.

- Roaring Writers (RW) encourages writers to improve their skills.

Parentheses can help organize items in a paragraph.

- Diets fail because (1) food groups are excluded, (2) restrictions increase hunger, and (3) exceptions aren't counted.

Parentheses are useful in referencing a claim to biblical truth.

For a Christian audience, reference to a familiar passage might be a slight detraction from your message and could be left out, but if you think it's needed, show it in parentheses inside the period.

- Jesus often talked about the importance of love and said we should even be kind to our enemies (Matthew 5:33–34).

Square brackets show details missing from quoted text.

- [Jesus said,] "If you forgive others for the wrongs they have done, your heavenly Father will forgive you" (Matthew 6:14 TDB).

Avoid parentheses in stories.

In both fiction and nonfiction storytelling, we don't need the timeout interruption of parenthetical expressions. Either leave them out or find a way to include the information in the narrative.

Never use parenthetical expressions in dialogue as in this example: "You really ought to try Panchito's (the Mexican restaurant on McCullough)," Ramon said.

Know where the period goes.

The period is the strong punctuation mark that ends the complete sentence, so it usually goes outside the right parenthesis.

When a whole sentence falls inside parentheses, the period goes inside.

Period

Those who have sacrificed possessions, relationships, and pleasures so they can write stories about Christ working in their lives will receive a much greater benefit, as well as eternal life. — *Matthew 19:29*

A period is like the referee's whistle, a hard stop that momentarily ends play before we move on.

A period is needed in many places.

You might think we only need a period after completing a sentence with its subject, verb, object, and modifying phrases. Not really. Stop anytime. Whenever it sounds right. When the hard stress of the word blows a whistle and says you should come to a complete stop.

In ancient times, sentences were called "periods," meaning a "cycle." A subject meets a verb and travels forward with information and action until the punctuation calls for a stop.

One space after the period, please.

Back in the old typewriter days, people developed the habit of typing two spaces after the period. That need changed with the introduction of computers and proportional typefaces.

For more than thirty years, the standard has been "one space after the period," but old habits die slowly. Manuscripts with two spaces aren't that unusual.

Quirks in word-processing programs can inadvertently add an extra space. Before submitting a manuscript, look professional by

121

doing a "find and replace," changing all occurrences of multiple spaces with a single space.

Brevity doesn't mean to abbreviate.

Periods are used for abbreviations. Back when print text was manually typeset one letter at a time, saving characters was important, and abbreviations were more common than they are today.

Brevity now means "the quickest path to the meaning." You don't want your busy reader to waste a microsecond figuring out what an abbreviation stands for.

A few abbreviations are considered the correct spelling of the way we talk. For example, we say, *Mr. and Mrs. Jones*, not *Mister and Mistress Jones*. You might say, *Dr. Frederick*.

When in doubt, err on the side of clarity, spelling out the word. Not everybody knows what *Gen.* means. Always spell out the books of the Bible, because many people don't know who *Mat.* is.

For Junior and Senior in names, we can now have Jr and Sr as a part of the name, without the period. The District of Columbia is now spelled DC like other states, and the United States can be spelled US, without the periods.

- While at West Texas Military Academy, **General** Douglas MacArthur played quarterback on the football team.
- In Matthew 4:7, Jesus says one should not test God.
- John Roberts Jr became the seventeenth chief justice of the US Supreme Court.
- The US capitol is in Washington, DC.

Periods go *inside* quotation marks.

Unlike colons and semicolons, which always go *outside*, the period always goes *inside* the quotation marks.

- After so many books, I didn't need to read "How to Write." I just needed to write.

Question Mark

*Blessed are humble writers, those who are content with
who they are, for they will discover their unique voice
that resonates with their audience. — Matthew 5:5*

A question is a stop in play to express doubt or uncertainty about something. It demands time to consider the possibilities and try to find an answer.

Questions are essential tools for writers to put the outcome in doubt and make readers want to find out what the next play will be.

Know where the mark belongs.

Of course, doesn't everybody know that a question mark belongs at the end? Yes, but at the end of what? Usually, it's at the end of the sentence—but not always.

If the entire sentence is a question, then the mark belongs at the end of the sentence. But that can be confusing when we have dialog that might or might not be a question and might or might not be at the end of the sentence.

With dialog in the sentence, does the question mark go inside or outside the quotation marks? It all depends.

(1) A statement containing dialog that's a question.

In this case, the question mark belongs *inside* the quotation marks, at the end of the question. When the dialog ends the sentence, there is no punctuation outside the quotation marks.

- Hunter said, "Are you sure?"
- Faith said, "How can I believe that?" and walked out the door.

(2) A question containing dialog that is a statement.

In this case, the question mark ends the sentence, not the dialog.

If the dialog falls at the end of the sentence, the quoted statement ends without punctuation, and the question mark is placed *outside* the quotation. The sentence, not the dialog, forms the question.

- Who said, "Men go where angels fear to tread"?
- Did Ruth say, "I don't want to go," when she really did want to go?

(3) A question contains dialog that is a question.

In this case, you might have two question marks inside the same sentence. The question mark belongs *inside* the quotation marks, at the end of the question. When the dialog ends the sentence, there is no punctuation outside the quotation marks.

- Did the teacher say, "What is the answer?" when she knew the answer?
- Why does everyone keep asking, "Why are we going?"

Beware the question that looks like a statement.

Spanish punctuates questions with a mark at both the beginning and the end: *¿hablas español?* Before the first word, we already know a question is being asked. But in English, readers can be shocked when they reach the end of a sentence and learn that what they thought was a statement was a question.

- You didn't have to go to the store before you prepared dinner?
- Thomas Jefferson wrote the Declaration of Independence to say that God made everyone alike?

The longer the sentence, the more likely that readers might be confused with a question they thought was a statement. To fix that potential problem, reword the sentence so the question is obvious from the beginning.

- Didn't you have to go to the store before you prepared dinner?
- Why did Thomas Jefferson write the Declaration of Independence? Was it to say that God made everyone alike?

Distinguish statements from questions.

You can't always trust grammar-checking software. Sentences that end with *what*, *why*, or *how* are not always questions.

- Guess what. I've decided not to go.
- Al didn't make it to work. I wonder why.

If a question is intended, be sure it's a question.

- Can you believe it? I've decided not to go.
- Al didn't make it to work. I have to wonder, why?

For longer sentences, be sure a question is obvious from the beginning. Short sentences can change from statement to a question simply by changing the punctuation.

- Daryl is going to the rodeo.
- Daryl is going to the rodeo?

Quotation Marks

You can be sure your present pain is nothing
compared to the value of a finished manuscript
when it is published. — Romans 8:18

Quotation marks identify titles that won't stand alone, spoken dialog, and words quoted from other speakers and writers.

Know when to go single.

Use single quotes for quotations inside dialogue. Use double quotes when writing quotations of what someone has said or written, converting any double quotes within the quotation to single quotes.

- Kyle said, "I believe it was Abraham Lincoln who said, 'Ballots are the peaceful successors to bullets.'"

Use quotes to change the meaning.

Quotation marks may be used to signify irony or reservation, a departure from the normally understood meaning. For foreign words and words used as words themselves, use italics, not quotes.

- I suppose you think these are "normal" people.
- You must feel better about no "new" taxes.
- Since the word *surreptitiously* isn't familiar to many people, why don't you use the more-common *deceptively?*

Semicolon

As we focus on the Lord's presence and write for his glory, all who give themselves to the craft are changed into his image, rising from one publishing success to the next as the Holy Spirit keeps working in our lives. — 2 Corinthians 3:18

The comma with a dot on top is a long pause or a short stop, which isn't of much use anymore. But it still has a few important uses.

Scrap the old style.

The old practice of using a semicolon instead of a conjunction to link closely related clauses isn't understood by many of today's readers. A hundred years ago, you might be praised for writing a sentence that covered half a page. Today, you'll be thanked for short paragraphs, short sentences, and lots of white space on the page.

Consider using either a period for a complete stop or a dash for a long pause.

Know the important uses.

A semicolon separates list items that include commas.

- On her tour, she stopped at Wichita, Kansas; Chicago, Illinois; and Louisville, Kentucky.

Since the comma separates verses of the Bible, a semicolon is used to separate chapters.

- Jesus talks about faith in Matthew 8:10, 26; 14:31; Luke 8:25; and 12:28.

Go *outside* the quotation marks.

Unlike periods and commas, which always go *inside*, the semicolon always goes *outside* the quotation marks.

- After so many books, I didn't need to read "How to Write"; I just needed to write.

Slash

I can write anything if Christ will give me the
ability and stamina. — Philippians 4:13

A slash is used to create either/or words and Uniform Resource
Locator (URL) website addresses.

Almost all uses are in nonfiction.

The slash in either/or words should rarely be used. Wherever
possible, use *or* instead of the slash. Most writers avoid *he/she*,
his/hers, and *him/her* as singular genderless pronouns. Writing *he or*
she, *his or hers*, or *him or her* is grammatically correct but awkward.

Switching from a singular to a plural sense might be the best
choice.

- If he/she doesn't know what to do, he/she can flip a coin.
- If he or she doesn't know what to do, he or she can flip a
  coin.
- If they don't know what to do, they can flip a coin.

Grammarians will now accept using the plural *they* or *their* in a
singular sense, which might be useful in some cases.

- If a person doesn't know what to do, they can flip a coin.

Fiction use is rare.

As a general rule, don't use slashes in storytelling. They will
naturally show up in the few cases where they are necessary.

- Before the accident, Tyler was an owner/operator for Jackson Trucking.
- William turned the dial on his AM/FM tube radio, still working since 1962.

Parts of Speech

*Whatever you write for people, make your message most
pleasing to the Lord, for the greatest reward comes from
publishing with him.* — *Colossians 3:23–24*

The meaning of a word changes when it is used in different ways.
What in the world is a *prepositional verb*? A table of examples can be
found in the Appendix.

> **If we know how our
> language works, we can
> make it work better.**

If you understand what the parts-of-speech functions are, you'll construct better sentences for better communication.

- **Adjectives** modify or clarify the meaning of nouns or pronouns. They cannot modify other adjectives without a unifying hyphen that makes the compound adjective function as a single modifier.
- **Adverbs** add meaning to a verb, but they can also modify adjectives and other adverbs.
- **Conjunctions** join words, phrases, and clauses in a relationship with one another, either in similarity or in contrast.
- **Interjections** are short expressions of emotion or sentiment, sometimes followed by an exclamation mark.
- **Nouns** are *things* that exist or do something—a person or place, perhaps—or something abstract, like an action, quality, thought, or feeling.

- **Prepositions** are usually pre-positioned to show a relationship between a noun, pronoun, or some other word or element in the rest of the sentence.
- **Pronouns** are a unique group of "pros" that function as nouns or noun representatives.
- **Verbs** describe action, state of being, or a condition in relation to what a noun is or does.

Blessed are writers who mourn, who grieve over their lack of success, for God will bring comfort, joy, and laughter to their aching hearts. — Matthew 5:4

Adjectives are like paintbrushes, coloring, clarifying, or quantifying nouns and pronouns. They cannot modify other adjectives without a unifying hyphen that makes the compound adjective function as a single modifier.

Make the picture clear.

In the hand of an unskilled artist, adjectives can leave a mess. Mark Twain said, "If you see an adjective, kill it," probably because most adjectives either say too much or too little.

Indefinite adjectives such as *many*, *short*, and *large* tell something about a noun without being exact. As you write, the word describes what you have in mind, but it's not specific enough for readers to create the same picture.

For example, how long is a *long* rope? You know it's six feet, but as far as readers know, it could be two feet, twenty feet, or fifty.

- Bill used a long rope to tether the cars' bumpers.
- Many friends visited Sally in the hospital.
- By late afternoon, they came to a very small river.

To be clear, avoid indefinite adjectives and be precise with the picture.

- Bill used a twelve-foot rope to tether the cars' bumpers.
- Three friends visited Sally in the hospital.
- By late afternoon, they came to a trickling creek.

Without a comparison, readers can't distinguish between *large, very large,* and *gargantuan.*

- Some large wolves surrounded the camp.
- Seven wolves as big as grizzly bears surrounded the camp.

The best adjectives show the picture instead of interpreting it.

- It was a beautiful day.
- It was a sunny, cool day.

Slash redundant modifiers.

An adjective that carries the same or nearly the same meaning weakens the expression.

- The ~~sum~~ total was 147.
- William used the ~~exact~~ same words in his speech.

The Appendix contains a table of redundant words.

Avoid adjectives that state the obvious.

After finishing your first draft, do a word search for throwaway words. The Appendix contains a table of throwaway words.

- ~~All~~ the boys gathered in a circle.
- On the way home, Paul had to stop and buy ~~some~~ drinks for the party.

An adjective modifying an adjective requires a hyphen.

Two adjectives can independently modify a noun, but a hyphen is needed to group adjectives when they collectively modify the noun. Test the need for a hyphen by eliminating the second adjective. If the sentence is still true, then the words independently modify the noun. No hyphen is needed.

Be sure you have the right adjective.

Anxious means "fearful apprehension," not eager anticipation. Should there be a distinction between *crucial* and *critical?* Is he the *eldest* or the *oldest?* Do you know the difference between *nude* and *naked?*

In the Shades of Meaning section in the Appendix, you'll find valuable help in selecting the right adjective.

Adverbs

Use plainly spoken words so people can easily read my message and run to tell others. — Habakkuk 2:2

Adverbs add meaning to a verb, but they can also modify adjectives and other adverbs. However, their frequent use is a sign of weak, lazy writing.

Use strong verbs showing action without need for adverbs.

Since the verb is the focus of the action, a modifier can distract rather than give support.

- Herb gently patted her on the shoulder.
- Peter smiled slightly.
- He painstakingly worked his way through the crowd.

Because patting is gentle, the verb is stronger if we leave out the adverb. How slight was Peter's smile. Was it a smirk, a grin, or what? When a person "works his way," it's obviously done *painstakingly*.

Search your manuscript for all the *-ly* adverbs. Most of the time, their deletion will make the existing verb stronger.

- Herb patted her on the shoulder.
- Peter smiled.
- He worked his way through the crowd.

If you think the adverb is necessary, then consider using a different verb or adding a metaphor that would create a better picture, with no need for the adverb. If Peter smiled sadly, the adverb does well at adding meaning to the verb. You might want to keep that one.

Use adverb inspection as a yellow flag to make the words more specific to the picture you want readers to create in their minds. That's extra work, because you need to re-imagine the situation and decide what the pat, smile, or walk was like. That effort will pay off in more than the improved sentence. The more you do it, the more that your first draft will use better words with fewer adverbs.

- Herb patted her shoulder as if her fourth-place loss had been a victory.
- Peter smiled like he knew something she didn't know.
- He pushed, retreated, and jostled his way through the crowd.

Cut the adverb by including its concept in the verb.

Actions are always stronger when they can be expressed in fewer words.

- The boys talked quietly among themselves.
- In a stupor, Tim walked erratically toward the bar.
- Steven thought intensely about the situation.

What verb might we use to include the concept of the adverb?

- The boys whispered among themselves.
- In a stupor, Tim stumbled toward the bar.
- Steven contemplated the situation.

Eliminate most qualifiers.

A weak adjective isn't improved with an adverb. Two times zero is still zero. Two times *weak* spells *doubly weak*. We don't strengthen *weak* by adding *weakness*. Leave out the adverb weakness, and your words are a little stronger.

- The weather was simply too hot for outside activities.

- John is absolutely my best friend.
- I was literally exhausted.
- Suddenly I felt like a hundred pounds had been lifted off my shoulders.
- Finally I gave up.

Is there a difference between "too hot" and "simply too hot"? If a best friend isn't *absolutely* best, she wouldn't be the best, would she? What distinguishes literal exhaustion from exhaustion? All feelings come suddenly, and giving up is final.

These adverbs are weak qualifiers and should be left out.

- The weather was too hot for outside activities.
- John is my best friend.
- I was exhausted.
- I felt like a hundred pounds had been lifted off my shoulders.
- I gave up.

Avoid adverbs in dialog tags.

The information desired from the adverb is obvious in the dialog. It should be left out.

- "Don't even think about it," Sam shouted angrily.
- "I get to go to camp," Susie said gleefully. "I get to go to camp."
- "I don't think I can make it," Dylan said doubtfully.
- "You don't know what you're doing," Mom said judgmentally.
- "The world will end tomorrow," the bum said cataclysmically.

If not obvious, the adverb is weak, telling rather than showing. Use actions, tone of voice, or body language in a separate sentence to identify the speaker and add meaning to what is said.

- "Don't even think about it." Sam raised both hands like he was stopping traffic.
- "I get to go to camp." Susie beamed as she twirled in a short dance. "I get to go to camp."
- "I don't think I can make it." Dylan looked like he had already failed.
- "You don't know what you're doing." Mom sounded like his teacher when he hadn't been listening.
- "The world will end tomorrow." The bum looked about ready for the grave.

Conjunctions

God's word is a lamp that lights my writing journey. — *Psalm 119:105*

Conjunctions join words, phrases, and clauses in a relationship with one another, either in similarity or in contrast.

Separate a conjunction for emphasis.

You may have heard in school that a sentence should *never* begin a sentence. That is generally true, because *and* should not be used to flow from one thought or event to the next. But there are exceptions. And there are times when the word at the beginning is important for emphasis.

- I ran a marathon for the first time. And I won.
- Bill loved hard work. But not all the time.

Never put a comma after a conjunction.

Since the conjunction's function is to join, a comma after a conjunction is counter-productive. This mistake happens most frequently when the conjunction is used to begin a sentence.

Why might you notice commas after conjunctions in bestselling books? Perhaps the writer or editor didn't know the best practice. Or they might be using *and* or *but* as transition words when *therefore* or *however* would be the correct choice.

We never need a comma after *so*. Before the word, we want a comma when it means "therefore," but we do not want a comma when it means "in order that."

Know the reason for joining.

By knowing a conjunction's function, you form easily understood relationships between words, phrases, and clauses.

The most common conjunction, *and*, should join items to show similarity or something in common. The items on both sides of the conjunction should balance physically, logically, and grammatically.

- Bread *and* butter live a balanced life together, physically, logically, and grammatically.
- Bread *and* "the yellowish solid produced from churning cream" balance physically but not grammatically.
- Bread *and* laughter balance grammatically but not physically or logically.

We have *but* and *yet* to connect opposing items, with *yet* used to show remarkable contrast.

- I wanted to play basketball, but I was a midget among giants.
- She sat in a stadium full of people, yet felt very much alone.

We have *for* and *because* to link truth with its reason.

If the truth exists independent of the reason, we can delete the reason and the statement remains true. In that case, we have an *explanatory* phrase that is preceded with a comma.

- She couldn't keep her eyes open, for the lecture was terribly boring.
- John didn't go to the store, because it was closed for the holiday.

In *because* clauses, if the truth depends on the reason, we can't delete the reason without changing the truth of the statement. In that case, we have a *restrictive* phrase that is not preceded with a comma.

- Did you go because there was no reason not to go?

We have *or* and *nor* to show choices that we have or don't have.

- We can go to the movies or stay home and watch TV.
- With so much work to do, we can't go to the movies nor can we stay home and watch TV.

Words paired with a conjunction show a correlation between two items. The most common pairs are: *both/and, either/or, neither/nor, whether/or,* and *not only/but also.*

- Both a receiver and the defensive back were injured on the play.
- You should bring either a vegetable or a dessert to the potluck dinner.
- She had neither the opportunity nor the desire to compete in the beauty pageant.
- John couldn't decide whether to get up early or sleep late.
- The tornado destroyed not only the church but also the business three miles away.

Weigh in on the differences.

A long list of subordinating conjunctions modify the weight of the main clause. Here are some of them: *after, although, as, as long as, as soon as, as though, before, even if, if, inasmuch as, just as, now that, once, since, suppose that, that, though, until, when, whenever, wherever, which, while, who.*

- Whenever he could spare a few minutes, he would practice.
- Before Johnny could play, he had to clean his room.
- Even with a million dollars, he would still pick up a penny.
- After the power failure, John had to reboot his computer.

Blessed are shunned writers, those who are rejected, insulted, and falsely accused because of their Christian perspective. In their day of abuse, they will rejoice because their reward in Heaven is great. The ancient prophetic writers were treated the same way. — Matthew 5:11–12

Interjections are short expressions of emotion or sentiment, sometimes followed by an exclamation mark. They call timeout for an important announcement.

They can stand alone, without subject or verb, terminated with a period or exclamation mark. Or they can be one or more words within a sentence, set off with commas.

Exclaim with words, not punctuation.

When writers try to turn up the volume with exclamation marks, they miss the importance of letting the words do the talking instead of the punctuation. An exclamation mark is not a part of speech. It's a mark at the end of the words, saying, *By the way, those words you just read—those were supposed to be louder, so please back up and adjust your perception.*

Limit your use of exclamation marks to one-word shouts when a period seems unacceptable.

- Wow! I can't believe he did that.
- Oh no, I've locked my keys in the car.
- I enjoy my swimming pool, but good grief, hundred-degree water is way too hot.

*Writers do not hide their stories where they cannot
be read. They are published in emails, blogs, and
books to give light to everyone.* — *Matthew 5:15*

Nouns are *things* that exist or do something—a person or place,
perhaps—or something abstract, like an action, quality, thought,
or feeling. They have the most importance when they do
something, even if it's no more than to hold barbed wire or
display a *No Trespassing* sign.

Your choice of nouns makes a difference in whether your story
delivers boring news or a life-changing experience.

Use concrete nouns.

Readers won't fall and skin their knees on *abstract* nouns like
disapproval, courage, or *sensitivity.* Such words exist only in the mind.
Since they can't be recognized with the physical senses, they lead
to theoretical scenarios rather than real pictures.

A beginner might write: *Fear flowed through his veins.* Since the
writer senses the character's fear, readers are expected to feel the
same emotion, but they don't. In the words they read, they need
to see, hear, and touch the circumstance that caused the fear.

Be specific with your nouns.

You're looking for nouns that create the quickest, most vivid
picture. A specific noun is better than a general noun and
adjective.

In a deep point of view, you're the main character, present in the scene, not a telling reporter who might not be sure. Using a general noun like *dog, vehicle,* or *tree* keeps readers from being visually engaged, a part of the scene.

A big difference exists between a *dog, Chihuahua,* and a *Rottweiler.*

- Billy knelt to pet the neighbor's dog.
- Matt drove his friend's vehicle to work.
- Trees lined both sides of the country lane.

A vehicle could be a pickup, car, or army tank. Climbing a tree is different for a scrawny mesquite compared to a tall pine or California's towering sequoia.

- Billy stepped back, not sure what would happen if he tried to pet the Doberman Pinscher.
- Matt drove his stick-shift Ford Pinto to work.
- Weeping willows lined both sides of the country lane.

A rose is best-known by its name.

For the best visuals, ask yourself, *What kind is it?* and find nouns that more-perfectly fit the picture.

A thesaurus might be helpful, but you're not just looking for a *different* word. You're looking for a *better* word. Google "red rose" to see the Damask, Eden, or Beach rose. Naming a "Mr. Lincoln" rose doesn't have to be understood. Just the name will give readers a feeling of being there.

The www.OneLook.com website is an excellent resource for finding words within the same area. Search that site with **:snow,* and you'll find long lists of related nouns, adjectives, verbs, and adverbs.

Like a mighty river, words will flow from the mouth
of those who believe in Christ. — *John 7:38*

Prepositions are usually pre-positioned to show a relationship between a noun, pronoun, or some other word or element in the rest of the sentence. They link their object's relationship to the rest of the sentence relevant to time, space, or logic.

Choose the right preposition.

Jumping *in* the shower is much different from jumping *into* the shower. If your character is already in place, the action takes place *in*, but if moving from somewhere outside, the action is *into*.

- Getting soaked all over, Bonnie was jumping in the shower, singing joyfully.
- Leticia quickly undressed and jumped into the shower.
- Julia threw the wrapping into the trash.

Sitting *across* the table isn't the same as *beside* or *with* the table. Picture the relationship. Then choose the preposition that works best.

Pay attention to each phrase's placement in the sentence.

A prepositional phrase should be placed next to what it modifies.

- The patient was sent to a specialist with severe abdominal pain.

- William purchased a three-story house with a large office that had a basement.
- John spent thirty minutes to read the contract that his attorney had sent to him with his family.

The specialist wasn't the one who needed a doctor, the large office didn't have a basement, and the family wasn't sent with the contract.

- The patient with severe abdominal pain was sent to a specialist.
- William purchased a three-story house with a large office in the basement.
- John spent thirty minutes with his family to read the contract that his attorney had sent to him.

More isn't always better.

One is good, two might be okay, but a chain of more than three prepositional phrases can be difficult to follow. Numerous relationships become confusing. Try two sentences or explanatory phrases that don't require a preposition.

- After a week of wondering what to do, I was sitting in the office of a psychiatrist, filling out forms while looking for someone with the ability to analyze the situation, to diagnose my condition, and to write a prescription for the right medication.
- What could I do? The next week, I was sitting in a psychiatrist's office, filling out forms, looking for someone who could diagnose my condition and prescribe the right medication.

Convert prepositional phrases to adjectives or possessive nouns.

A single-word modifier is often better than a prepositional phrase.

- She lives in Atlanta but spends most of her time in the summer at her cottage in Massachusetts.
- The Ten Commandments were written by the finger of God on two tablets of stone.

When you see several prepositional phrases, look for ways to reword the sentence with only one or two.

- She lives in Atlanta but spends most of the summer at her Massachusetts cottage.
- God wrote the Ten Commandments on two tablets of stone.

Like city lights on a hill that cannot be hidden, your testimony should give light to the whole world. — Matthew 5:14

Pronouns are a unique group of "pros" that function as nouns or noun representatives. They are like *ambassadors*, representing *someone* or some *thing*.

Without a clearly understood *antecedent*—the noun that identifies *he, she,* or *it*—the ambassador has no one to represent other than himself, which is weak writing.

Watch for unclear antecedents.
You want readers to associate *he* or *she* with the right person and *it* with the right thing. Don't let readers be confused by a second possibility.

- John sat with Bill at the back of the church. He picked up a hymnal and turned to the responsive readings.
- As they neared the dock, they assured the ice skater that it was safe.

Who picked up the hymnal, John or Bill? Was the ice skater worried about the dock or the thickness of the ice?

- John sat at the back of the church with Bill, who picked up a hymnal and turned to the responsive readings.
- As they neared the dock, they assured the skater that the ice was safe.

Put the antecedent first.

When the point of focus is clearly upon one person, avoid using *he* or *she* at the beginning of a paragraph and then following with the person's name later on. As long as another character isn't introduced, the pronoun after the noun should be good for the entire paragraph.

- She stared at him. Rachel knew men, and everything about his expression said he was telling the truth.
- Rachel stared at him. She knew men, and everything about his expression said he was telling the truth.

Distinguish *who* from *that*.
Use *who* when referring to people.

- I was seen by the same doctor who had seen my student.
- We need to reach people who aren't part of the club.

Use *that* when referring to non-human entities. For a children's story that gives animals the ability to talk, use *who*.

- The bear who came last said, "Who ate my porridge?"
- This swamp is owned by the company that built the roads through the park.

Use *it* with caution.
Whenever *it* is used, view *it* as a yellow caution flag signaling where you might strengthen your writing. Readers have little difficulty visualizing the person that *he* or *she* refers to. The genderless *it* is a different matter.

It can be animal, vegetable, or mineral, real or abstract, human or spirit. With limitless possibilities, readers work to understand what *it* is.

For clarity and easier reading, strive to replace *it* with whatever *it* is.

- To reduce the cost of the reservoir, the Army Corps of Engineers moved it south.

- He bolted out of the chair and got the glass of water. He handed it to her.

Is the cost or the reservoir being moved? Did he hand her the glass or the chair? If you must use *it*, be sure the meaning of *it* is clear. A second sentence using *it* can often be combined with the previous sentence where *it* has been defined, eliminating the need for the pronoun.

- To reduce the cost, the Army Corps of Engineers moved the reservoir location to the south.
- He bolted out of the chair and handed the glass of water to her.

Know *which* from *that*.

Choosing the correct relational pronoun depends on whether the subsequent phrase *explains* or *restricts* the antecedent. For explanations, use *which*, preceded by a comma. For restrictions, use *that* with no comma.

These examples restrict:

- Smallmouth bass stirred the surface like whitewater rapids, striking the shad that were feeding on the algae.
- Kindness is a language that even the deaf can hear, a picture that even the blind can see.

These examples explain:

- The album was titled *And Then I Wrote*, Willie Nelson's first album, which included "Touch Me," "Crazy," "Hello Walls," and "Mr. Record Man."
- My convertible, which has a torn top, doesn't drive well in the rain.

For people, we use *who*, not *which* or *that*. Use a comma when the *who* phrase explains, no comma when it restricts.

- I talked to the guard who was standing outside the entrance.

- My best friend, who is ten years my senior, gives great advice.

The objective *whom* is being used less and less in everyday speech. When it falls immediately after a preposition, *whom* is still a common practice.

- To whom it may concern:

But in other situations, *whom* or even *that* might be preferred.

- Who did you give that to?
- When I look in the mirror, I see the same person that I saw yesterday.

When the meaning is still clear, the preference is to leave out the relational pronouns *whom* and *that*.

- When I look in the mirror, I see the same person I saw yesterday.

Decide what to do for a person's genderless singular pronoun.

The English language doesn't have a genderless singular pronoun for use instead of *he or she*, *his or hers*, or *him or her*. Writing *he or she*, *his or hers*, or *him or her* is grammatically correct but awkward.

- If he or she has the right answer, he or she doesn't have to ask.

Referring to a person who might be male or might be female as an *it* hasn't been accepted. For centuries, the male pronoun was used in a genderless sense, but modern society views that practice as sexist.

Most writers avoid *he/she*, *his/hers*, and *him/her* as singular genderless pronouns, but you may see it in nonfiction narrative. For storytelling, it's a bad idea.

- If he/she has the right answer, he/she doesn't have to ask.

Nonfiction works sometimes use either *he* or *she* interchangeably at random, where the examples could just as easily apply to the opposite sex. That practice can be confusing.

- If a person has the right answer, she doesn't have to ask. If he doesn't know, he can flip a coin.

Using *they* or *their* in the singular sense is now considered acceptable. We hear that structure frequently in everyday speech, even among professionals.

- If a person has the right answer, they don't have to ask.

The best approach converts the singular subject to plural so both the subject and pronoun are in full grammatical agreement. If the plural approach won't work in a situation and you can't rewrite the sentence without need for the pronoun, use of *they* or *their* might be the best choice.

- If they have the right answer, they don't have to ask.

*Blessed are those who strive to write their best,
who hunger and thirst to please God, for they
will find true satisfaction.* — Matthew 5:6

Verbs describe action, state of being, or a condition in relation to what a noun is or does.

Keep the action going.

In our cinematic world, readers are engaged through action verbs, not freeze-frame passive sentences. Nobody wants to spend an hour waiting in line or turn through a hundred pages in a book before they get to the action. From the first sentence, you want readers to live the story.

Action verbs should move readers rapidly forward on a roller-coaster ride of thrills, romance, drama, mystery, and suspense.

Passive voice isn't always bad.

You may have heard that use of the state-of-being verbs *is*, *am*, *was*, and *were* should be avoided at all cost. That's not true. Sometimes those plain verbs are essential.

The best definition of "passive" is "not active." Instead of moving forward, the subject receives instead of doing the action.

- Active: John hit the ball.
- Passive: The ball was hit by John.

In this case, *active* is better because the action moves forward instead of backward. Sentences are read from left to right, and readers would rather see the action move in the same direction.

Sometimes, the doer has no importance, is unknown, or should not be identified. In that case, we must have the passive voice without revealing the doer.

- The man was shot twice in the chest.
- Jerusalem was in turmoil over rumors of a newborn king.

Many assume that passive voice is telling, not showing. You may have heard many times that we always want to show. Not necessarily. When readers feel a desperate need for the information, what we would otherwise identify as telling becomes an important form of showing.

An ongoing action is sometimes the correct description.

An active verb should not displace what must be an ongoing action that is expressed with the passive *was* and the *-ing* verb form. What is often regarded as passive can be the correct visual of an ongoing action.

- When his father walked in, Timmy was sitting in the corner.
- When his father walked in, Timmy sat in the corner.

In the first example, Timmy is already seated when his father walks in. In the second example, Timmy finds a seat afterward.

- Pete was buttoning his shirt.
- Pete buttoned his shirt.

Since Pete took little time to button his shirt, the second example is better.

Beware the past-perfect *had* verbs.

Anytime we tell something that has already happened, we've become passive, taking readers away from the action that moves the story forward.

- Penny had dyed her hair blonde.
- Sergeant Andrews had found plenty of clues but still had no suspects.

What can we do to make these sentences presently active, without "had"? Make the truth current in dialog. With an introductory phrase, bring the past into present action.

- "Penny," Mark said, "when did you become a blonde?"
- With plenty of clues, Sergeant Andrews frantically searched for suspects.

Use introductory participial phrases with caution.

An ongoing action described in an introductory phrase must coincide in the same place and time and be of the same duration as the main action of the sentence.

The following examples are impossible, because they can't happen at the same time.

- Turning the corner, Fred walked past the store and down the alley.
- Swinging the golf club, she watched the ball hook to the right, bounce down the fairway, and find the sand trap.

We can fix the problem by making converting the participial phrase to begin with a preposition.

- After turning the corner, Fred walked past the store and down the alley.
- After swinging the golf club, she watched the ball hook to the right, bounce down the fairway, and find the sand trap.

Successive actions are often best-described in order as they happen.

- Fred turned the corner, went past the store, and walked down the alley.
- She swung the golf club and watched the ball hook to the right, bounce down the fairway, and find the sand trap.

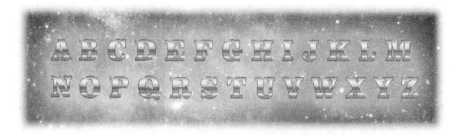

Capitalization

*Please understand, if you listen to God's Spirit within,
you will write to please him and to benefit others, not
to satisfy your selfish desires.* — *Galatians 5:16*

We capitalize proper nouns and most words in titles. Names are capitalized, but terms of affection or endearment are not. Days, months, and holidays are capitalized, but the seasons aren't. Understand the principles behind the main rules, and you'll have a good feel for what should or shouldn't be capitalized.

Adjectives formed from proper nouns usually aren't capitalized.

Continents, countries, and ethnic names are an exception.

- A Japanese citizen can be proud to be American.
- Some Hispanic people are not of Mexican descent.

Capitalize the names of regions and territories.

If the name of an area is called by name, capitalize. Adjectives and generic nouns are not capitalized.

- Geese fly south in the winter.
- The South has a warmer climate.
- The Johnsons live in West Texas.

When in doubt, look it up. The OneLook.com website may show different dictionaries that don't all agree. If you're writing for a publisher, you may be bound by the choice of a particular publisher. But for your own publishing, you get to choose what works best for your audience. Sometimes an internet search can tell you what's most commonly used, when dictionaries do not.

Capitalize relationships only when they replace a person's name.

Relationships like *dad*, *brother*, and *uncle* are lowercased when used generically or when preceded by a modifier.

- My daddy used to spend a lot of time with me.
- When Daddy is busy, he doesn't like interruptions.
- Did you tell your uncle John about the accident?
- I think Uncle John will be happy with my college choice.
- My son doesn't care anything about fishing.
- Listen to me, Son, and you'll save yourself a lot of grief.

The same rule applies to nicknames, professional titles, and terms of endearment like *sugar*, *honey*, or *darling*. Lowercase them unless they replace a person's name. Sometimes a generic label works well lowercased in quotes.

- How many home runs did Babe Ruth hit in his career?
- When Charlie was little, we often called him spunky.
- He was known as "the man."
- Jackson was captain of the team.
- Just tell me what to do, Captain, and it's done.

Lowercase titles when they are not part of the name.

- You should know that President Lincoln was the sixteenth president of the United States.

When titles of the armed forces are not capitalized, they are understood as generic descriptions, not an official title.

- The air force, army, and navy have different combat responsibilities.
- He's a marine, not an airman.

- Tim joined the National Guard.

Academic courses and degrees are lowercased unless they are the official name.

That's true for books and articles, but on formal documents like diplomas, resumés, and business cards, course names and degrees are usually capitalized.

- I took a great marketing class called Count Your Chickens.
- Francis has a master's degree in business administration.
- John graduated from Harvard with a Doctor of Philosophy degree.

Know when to capitalize pronouns referring to God.

Consistency is the rule. If you choose to capitalize, you can face major editing challenges in catching every time that *he, his, who, whose, whom, one, you, your, my, mine, myself, himself,* or *yourself* refers to God, Jesus, or the Holy Spirit.

Most of the modern Bible translations *do not* capitalize, including the CEV, ESV, KJV, MSG, NAS, NCV, NET, NIV, NLT, NRS, TEV, and TLB. If you choose to capitalize but you quote a translation that doesn't, the rule of consistency is violated. *The Chicago Manual of Style, The Christian Writer's Manual of Style, Words Into Type,* and *The Associated Press Style Manual* lowercase all pronouns referring to God.

Some Christians think lowercasing the pronouns shows a lack of reverence, which is not far removed from the Jewish practice of always spelling G-d for God.

The broad audience of believers, many of whom are seekers and new converts, didn't grow up with a prejudice for capitalizing and find the lowercase text easier to read.

If you're writing for a certain publisher, follow their preference or ask if they'll allow for an exception. For your self-published works, you get to choose. Just be consistent.

Capitalize religious terms when understood as proper names.

The word *church* might be capitalized when it refers to the Body of Christ. *Scripture* is capitalized when it refers to the Bible or God's Word but not when it refers to verses or passages.

Adjectives are not capitalized.

- The apostle Paul wrote most of the New Testament letters.
- By definition, messianic prophecies are about the Messiah.
- The best source for biblical truth is the Bible.

The stylebooks may say *kingdom, earth, heaven,* and *hell* should be lowercased, but when the word names the place where we live, that rule doesn't work well. When Earth names our planet in the same way that we name Mars, capitalization makes sense.

- The Bible promises believers eternal life in a heavenly kingdom called the Kingdom of Heaven.
- For as long as we live on Earth, we will walk on the earth.
- Where in hell did you get the idea that Hell is real?
- For heaven's sake, what do you mean?

In titles and headings, important words are capitalized.

Figuring out which words are most important can be difficult, because it's not a matter of lowercasing the short words and capitalizing all the others. If in doubt about the rules or you're not sure what counts as important, try the free conversion website at CapitalizeMyTitle.com, where you can select the rules from different style resources, including the *Associated Press Stylebook* and *The Chicago Manual of Style.*

Usually, we capitalize the first and last words and always the first word after a colon or dash. We capitalize all other words except for the articles *a, an,* and *the,* prepositions, and coordinate conjunctions like *and, but,* and *for.* But we do capitalize the conjunctions *When, If, That,* and *So.*

This is a style issue, and sometimes styles are a matter of personal taste. So about the time you think you know all the rules, you'll see a title that breaks a rule. You may even see a title or subtitle with none of the words capitalized.

Never use all caps.

As if overuse of exclamation marks is not enough, some writers feel compelled to use all-caps, bold face, or underline for emphasis. That's a bad idea, a practice that is often seen as a sign of novice writing.

We have only two ways to add emphasis to a word or phrase: italics or quotation marks.

- Did he *really* say that?
- She was desperate to win, to be "queen for the day."

Is there ever a situation where you might need all-caps? Perhaps when you wanted to describe the message on a sign or billboard. If you insist, at least use small caps, not the all-caps that should.

- I ignored the DETOUR sign and kept driving.
- The billboard said THINK. Inebriated Billy thought it said DRINK and turned into the next bar.

You might see morning and night indicated with AM, PM, A.M. or P.M. The best approach is the lowercase a.m. and p.m.

Spelling

*Be gracious with your stories, flavoring your
message with that which will answer the hunger
in everyone's heart. — Colossians 4:6*

The way we say things may seem to stay the same, but look ten
years back and you'll see differences. Language is constantly
changing, which includes spelling.

The *internet* used to be capitalized, but now it's considered a
generic lowercased term. In another ten years, it may simply be
known as the *net*.

Don't become spellcheck dependent.

Is spellcheck one word or two? Or is it hyphenated? When people
speak, do we call it *dialogue* or *dialog*? Do we send an
acknowledgement or an *acknowledgment*? In church, are people
worshipping or *worshiping*?

Spellcheck programs won't always tell us what is correct. It
won't catch the wrong word or the right word in the wrong place.
Even if we knew the preferred spelling, it might change next
week.

The best thing you can do is tell yourself that spelling is
important. Believe that, and you will pay attention to the way
words are most commonly spelled today, which will help you
write a better first draft.

Let misspelling and misuse of words bother you.

At one time, the Winnie the Pooh ride at Disney World had Pooh Bear saying, "Do you have anymore honey?" If you were there, might you have been the one person out of a hundred thousand who would notice that Pooh actually said, "Do you have any more honey"? Maybe somebody noticed, because that line isn't there anymore.

If you're a serious writer, you are listening to what public figures are saying on radio and TV, noticing what isn't said right or could have been said better. When you read advertisements, you see what works well and what doesn't. Poorly written novels become difficult to read, because you want to stop and reword the paragraph.

Your goal should be storytelling at its best.

Whether fiction or nonfiction, no truth can be expressed better and more memorably than with a captivating story. Readers remember stories much better than theological exposition or historical facts.

You are the only one who can tell your stories the way you need to tell them. Editors can make your message better, but better than

> A wrong word here or there isn't fatal—unless you have enough to be noticed.

what? They might move your manuscript from very bad to bad, from bad to fair, from fair to good, from good to great, from great to excellent, or just maybe, against all odds, you could have a bestseller.

Don't insist on perfection at the beginning.

First, get the message down. Then get the words right. While you write, worrying about grammar and spelling can impede your progress. Give your thoughts free flow to the page, doing your best to avoid any kind of interruption, not the phone, email, or taking time to look up a word.

For most audiences, your writing voice will be better if it resembles how you talk rather than the literary style you learned in school. Simple, conversational words are better than sounding like a preacher or an attorney.

At the first-draft level, just respect the squiggly red lines from spellcheck that says the dictionary doesn't recognize the word. Fix or accept those and move on.

Watch for sometimes-confused spelling.

Here are a few words that sound alike or are in some way similar and easily confused, so they can be mindlessly typed incorrectly:

- they, they're, their
- to, too, two
- its, it's

In the Appendix under Shades of Meaning, you will find a long list of sometimes-confused words. Know the distinctions, and your first draft will be better.

Story Killers

God has chosen our meager writing skills to impact readers more than bestselling authors. He has chosen our small, insignificant words to change lives that were thought to be unchangeable. — 1 Corinthians 1:27

To improve our writing skills, we need to know what to do. We can also be helped by knowing what *not* to do.

Avoid suspense, mystery, romance, and humor.

A hundred years ago, newspapers thrived with human interest stories on the front page. Novels were serialized with another chapter in each issue, so people never wanted to miss reading their copy from front to back. They didn't mind the small advertisements scattered throughout.

> The *what* without the *how* and *why* is a boring news report.

Then the newspaper managers wised up. The front page was reserved for breaking news with shocking headlines. Articles were grouped into sections so sports enthusiasts didn't have to be bothered by anything else. All the advertisements moved to their own section that was sometimes thicker than the rest of the newspaper.

What brought a thriving industry into rapid decline?

Except for the small opinions column with prejudice that few people cared anything about, news became no more than reporting what happened. Coupon clippers cared for nothing but the advertisements.

Suspense, mystery, and romance disappeared. There were no serialized novels. If people wanted more than the news, they would have to go somewhere else. And they did.

Just telling what happened is boring news—a bad idea. Fill your stories with all the suspense, mystery, romance, and humor.

Present the solution instead of the problem.

Let's cut to the chase. Give people the answers so they don't have to be bothered with the questions. Newspapers are filled with doom and gloom, which people don't like. So surely we should leave pain and suffering out of our stories.

For a refreshing escape from all the problems, let's have everything go right for a change.

Those who know the Lord are thrilled with the joy and peace that fills our hearts. The last thing we want to do is reveal our sordid pasts. Just tell people that God has changed our lives. Life is wonderful now. Don't include the terrible struggles that would make us relive our pain.

By presenting the solution instead of the problem, readers don't feel the need to keep turning the pages. Until we've adequately presented a crucial

> **Problems give the solution meaning.**

question, people aren't interested in our answers. Without a good picture of the darkness, readers can't appreciate the light.

The painful struggle makes the story. It gives the solution meaning. You can't leave that out without creating boring news, which few people want to read. But that's not the only reason you should relive your pain in telling your stories.

Your story has an exciting ending. The painful parts do more than refresh the past that you want to forget. It lets you live a even greater triumph at the end, when not only you but all your audience shout in victory.

Present the problem in all its infamy, and readers will praise you for the solution that now has meaning.

Avoid conflict.

With a strong desire to be accepted, appreciated, and loved, we naturally want to avoid conflict. However, that natural tendency is self-defeating.

> With conflict, we face either a stepping stone or a tombstone.

Great arguments settle conflicts. Silence never does. To keep the peace, people say they agree, when they really don't. Does that help the conflict? No, the conflict worsens, showing up in other areas.

All we need to face conflict is two people with different goals—like a marriage, which the honeymoon is always short. Our differences can be our strength when we face confrontation—or it can bring our demise when we don't.

Our inner conflicts are more heartrending than our physical battles. Everybody has them, so leaving them out leaves our stories unrealistic. Theoretically, you could have *too much* conflict and tension, but so far, nobody has been able to do that.

Conflict is essential to create a dilemma that leaves readers wondering what will happen next. You can't afford to leave it out.

Give too much information.

We live in an information age where survival depends on knowing. Yet technology has empowered us with not needing to know—not until the moment we need the information. Then we just Google to get it.

The best way to bore readers is to give them information that they see no need for. Include a lengthy setup and describe the

> Until it's needed, information is useless and therefore boring.

scene with intricate details about landscape, weather, and the social conditions of the day. Tell about the battle about to begin, what people want and why they are fighting.

Describe past battles and why they are relevant now. Include a bit of history and scientific fact, proof that the author did her research.

The best question you can ask is, "Why does this information matter?" If it matters to you but not the reader, you've succeeded in killing your story.

Any information is too much when the reader feels no need to know.

Create a vague picture.

A man lives in a house with a child, a dog, and a cat. He drives a vehicle to a job in the city, doing the same things each day. He looks forward to someone having a meal ready when he gets home, before he watches his favorite TV show. He will sleep somewhere in comfort, because he knows who he is, what he does, and what he wants.

> Vague pictures are easy to create, but they aren't exciting.

A quick story is easy when you don't have to decide what *things* are. A *person* can do *something* with *someone* without having to describe what *everything* is. We can refer to *it* as if it were *something* when it's really *nothing* at all.

If you care enough about your story to avoid its death from the beginning, don't be vague with your descriptions. Use specific nouns and verbs that create a vivid picture of who your character is, what he does, and what he wants.

Always show kindness.

Your hero is perfect, always the champion for good. In every situation, she is considerate, honoring others and never saying an unkind word. Conflict doesn't bother her, because her desires don't matter when they conflict with what someone else wants. She even loves her enemies.

If you want to kill your story, let your hero remain the same. Readers don't like heroes who have no flaws and win every

> Syrup on pancakes is good, but not everywhere—not spaghetti, tacos, or mashed potatoes.

battle because they're so smart and strong. Why? Because readers are nothing like that. They want to identify with the hero, changing through the unpredictable experience of story, surviving a battle that appeared most likely would be lost.

Explain the situation.

People love puzzles for the thrill of figuring them out. While sharpening their minds by having to think, they find comfort in knowing they aren't as dumb as others might believe. If you want to kill those rewards, tell readers what your characters are feeling.

Give her the answer to number four down, a five-letter word for *alike*, with a third-letter *T*. Will the word *patch* work? Maybe. It works with the word across that ends with *H*. But the *P* won't fit with anything she can imagine for the other crossword.

> When nothing is left to the imagination, readers fall asleep.

Readers are smart. When all the clues come together, the answer will be rewarding, even if they don't figure it out.

To avoid killing your story, give no interpretation or explanation. Create lots of mystery and suspense with a heavy dose of conflict and tension, sprinkled with humor and romance, and readers will enjoy turning the pages to reach the answers at the end.

Make the outcome predictable.

In sports, fans are captivated by the game for only as long as they care about who's playing and the outcome is in doubt. If you want fans to leave early, let them feel like no great plays are left to be made. The outcome is certain. They might as well do something else.

> The game is important as long as fans don't know the score.

If readers think they know what happens next, your story is facing sudden death long before the end. It's over unless you can keep them on the edge of their seats because something else could go wrong or there's still a chance for something going right. There might be overtime.

Trivialize the danger.

In the beginning, Superman was not a popular character. He could do all the things people can't do but love to dream what it would be like if they could. With a single leap, he can clear tall buildings. He's faster than a speeding train, and he flies like a plane. He lifts trucks like they are toys and can see through walls. But people didn't like him until kryptonite made him vulnerable and human like Clark Kent.

> If you want to kill your story, leave out the kryptonite.

A little danger from the red kryptonite was not enough. With the green variety, our hero might die. Blue, orange, and black kryptonite came with their unique threats to life. Other colors had special properties to make the danger real.

A story's strength is found in the struggle, which doesn't mean much unless you make it a life-or-death matter.

Make obstacles easy to overcome.

In the 1970s, people were introduced to the thrill of victory and the agony of defeat every Saturday on ABC television's *Wide World of Sports*. Every weekend, viewers saw ski jumper Vinko Bogataj tumble head over heels like a rag doll and crash into the barrier. He became a stunning icon for the great risks we face to reach lofty goals.

> When nothing is at risk, victory is meaningless.

For no more than the *hope* of winning, Olympic athletes sacrifice their bodies at an insane level. Their greatest victories come at the greatest cost.

Stepping stones are too easy. Make them stumbling blocks.

If you want to kill your story, don't let your hero fall. Readers expect him to win the prize, so wouldn't it be good to thrill them with the coveted gold? No, they'll be disappointed if the "gold" turns out to be what they expected.

Repeat the same actions.

Jack said it before. He would naturally say the same thing again, right?

We know what Jill did when her boyfriend dumped her last time. If she's the same person, she should do the same thing now.

Every day while on a cruise, Hosea was awed by the pink, purple, and gold shades of the sunrise. On the second day that he captured the beauty on Facebook for his friends at home, he got no likes because they'd seen it before.

> Nothing is more boring than the same old thing.

If you want to kill the story, keep describing the sun and miss the rainbow on the opposite horizon. Follow the wisdom of Solomon by proving there's nothing new under the sun. Or you can show true-to-life variety that spices your story and keeps it from being bland.

When Jack and Jill do the same thing on the hill, nothing has changed, and that's a story-killer.

Make choices obvious.

For a choice to have value, readers must care about the situation and feel the pain of not knowing which way is best.

On a partly cloudy day, Jonathan took his son and daughter fishing in the bay. While anchored in deep water, far from the shore, high winds struck and capsized their boat. The waves pulled his son to the left, his daughter to the right, both gasping for air, unable to stay afloat. Jonathan could save one but not both. Which would it be?

> Equal and opposite unmet desires create dilemmas that matter.

If you let the solution be easy, your story is on life support and may die. Choosing between good and bad is much too obvious. Let your main character choose between two bad things.

Or let him choose the bad instead of the good, because he has no choice.

Create characters that act, talk, and believe alike.

If you want to kill your story, take the lazy approach. Let your characters think, talk, and act like you.

On the other hand, if you want true-to-life believable characters, be as intimately understanding of the villain as the hero. Identify with the vanquished as well as the victorious. Present someone's lie as if it were your own truth. When needed, switch from confident to despondent, because you are able to see the much different worlds of both the survivalist and the suicidal.

> People are about as much alike as a hissing cat and a barking dog.

Just for the next important scene, adopt the uncomfortable position of the stalker, the town bum, or the two-timing cheat you would never want to be.

Let readers think everything will be all right.

Readers want happy endings, but you can kill your story by making the outcome apparent from the beginning.

No matter who they are or how much they do or don't have, life is tough. They don't want to read about someone with no need for worry, because everything will be all right.

> Readers will be disappointed if happiness comes easily.

The cavalry can't ride in to save the day. If God will have to do a miracle, they first want to see all the reasons why that could never happen—and keep seeing why it can't until it makes perfect sense that it should. But it doesn't. It can't. Finally, when readers accept the reality that the miracle isn't happening, it does—but not in the way they could ever imagine.

Create no sense of urgency.

Floating down the river may be relaxing, but if she's not going somewhere for some reason, her story is a sleeping pill. If how she starts, what she does, or when she gets there doesn't matter, then what she wants has no sense of urgency. Without a deadline, there is no threat of dying. Without a threat, readers don't care.

172

Where is the bomb? Who will be killed? When will it explode? Such urgency can drive a story from beginning to end, keeping the pages turning.

In another story, there is no bomb. No one will be killed.

> **Without a sense of urgency, a ticking time bomb doesn't matter.**

There is no problem that can't wait until another day. This is good, right? Now we can relax and enjoy the day. We've also killed the story.

Miss the deadline, and he's sure to be fired. He must be at his presentation best. If he drops the ball, he's off the team and collecting unemployment. But if he doesn't need the money, what does it matter? Something else must make it matter, or the story is on life support.

Use uncommon words.

Trying to impress readers with our knowledge and writing skills is not a good idea. Between the language of a lawyer and an illiterate bum, look for common words that are readily understood by common people.

> **Fancy words and flowery phrases create the wrong impression.**

Our province is not to cognitively commove citizenry with luxuriant nomenclature. If we want to imbibe readers with our tarradiddle, we need a depiction so exculpated, compendious, and enrapturing that the words become microscopic.

What are we trying to say? Say it simply, and readers will understand. Our job is not to impress people with fancy words. If we want to engage readers with our stories, we need a picture so clear, concise, and captivating that the words become invisible.

Start slow.

Don't be fooled by bestselling novels that use the first fifty pages of information before readers can figure out what the main character wants and why it matters. Start with an explosive moment and escalate the tension from there.

> **Kill the setup, not the story.**

Practice Writing

Make good on your commitment to the Lord by preparing to share your experiences with those who might not understand how you have survived your struggles. Always be ready to reveal why you have hope in this tumultuous world. — 1 Peter 3:15

We may not think much of practice, but isn't that what everyone does until they get published? Therefore, if we want others to read our words, we do well to practice deliberately and frequently.

Make Time to Practice

Practice becomes painful as soon as we regard it as work. But if we choose to make it fun, we can eagerly embrace the opportunity each day. We won't have to *find* the time. We will *make* the time.

> **Unless we're perfect, we need to practice.**

Practice with Desire

Some have said, "Practice makes perfect." Really? True, we'll not get better without practice, but if we could practice perfectly, we wouldn't need to practice, would we? Since to some degree all practice is flawed, our imperfect practice can leave us unchanged—or even make us worse.

Only one kind of practice is guaranteed to make us better: practice with a *desire to improve*. With that vision, we will readily admit our weaknesses and keep seeking ways to grow our strengths.

Recognize the Value of Practice

If success were easy, it wouldn't be worth much. Talent is over-rated, an excuse for those who view themselves as something less than they could be.

Many people regard Mozart as a "child prodigy," as if what comes so difficultly for others came naturally to him as a youngster. Not so. From the time he could walk, he ate, slept, and breathed music. He copied the masters. He had a private tutor. By age twelve, he had more practice than most musicians experience in a lifetime.

What we see in others are the results of many hours of hard work. If we see the value, we'll do the work, causing those who haven't invested the time to recognize us as "talented."

Practice with Persistence

Bestselling authors have learned the value of persistence. They use time wherever they can, gathering ideas, making notes, and writing. Even with that effort, they will produce around 750 good words a day, about three double-spaced pages. At the same time, they might cut 2,000 bad words, because they insist on *good* words.

> Sharpened skills become dull without practice.

At such a slow daily output, how they can finish a novel in a year. They do it by writing every day. Do the math: five days per week, fifty weeks per year, equals 750 pages of 187,500 words. That's enough for two books in a year, yet most Christians don't write one in a lifetime.

Persistence in writing something, almost every day is much more productive than occasionally writing a lot.

Practice with Purpose

Writing instructors repeatedly encourage aspiring writers to read books in their genre and other books as well. That's wonderful advice, because we're sure to absorb some of what worked in bestselling fiction and nonfiction. But we also run the risk of absorbing what doesn't work.

Try this fifteen- to thirty-minute exercise once a week:

1. Read a page from a novel and pick your favorite paragraph.
2. Read the paragraph aloud.
3. Write the paragraph.
4. As the character, put yourself more deeply into the scene, and ask questions about how you could better describe what you're seeing.
5. Edit the paragraph, looking for ways to improve the sentences.
6. Using your own words, write how you would describe the scene.

Practice Example from *Intensity* by Dean Koontz

The red sun balances on the highest ramparts of the mountains, and in its waning light, the foothills appear to be ablaze. A cool breeze blows down out of the sun and fans through the tall dry grass, which streams like waves of golden fire along the slopes toward the rich and shadowed valley. In the knee-high grass, he stands with his hands in the pockets of his denim jacket, studying the vineyards below. As it slowly sinks behind the mountains, the sun sprays light so warmly colored and so mordant that, where touched, the darkening land appears to be wet with it and dyed forever.

After you've read the page silently, picked the paragraph, and read the paragraph out loud. Now be the character and put yourself more deeply into the scene. Ask questions about what you're visualizing. Why is the sun red? Can the sun bring a cool breeze? That seems to be a contradiction. Who is "he"? Where is he looking from? If the sun has sunk behind the mountains, how is it still spraying light? Will all readers know what mordant means? If not, they won't check the dictionary.

> Make practice fun, and it doesn't have to be work.

Edit and rewrite the sentences, looking for ways they could be improved.

The sun balances above the mountain peaks, setting the foothills ablaze. A cool breeze from the snowcaps fans the tall, dry grass in the valley, creating ocean-like waves with golden fire cresting on the shadows. Jack Simpleton leans against the railing on the bridge that spans the roaring rapids. As the sunlight fades, the colors glisten as if an artist had spread fresh paint on his canvas.

Using your own words, write how you would describe the scene.

Jack Simpleton leaned against the bridge railing, above the roaring rapids, wishing the day didn't have to end. The setting sun, just above the mountain peaks, gave the foothills their last breath of daylight. The breeze off the snowcaps cooled his face and warmed his heart. The tall, dry grass in the valley swayed like ocean waves, the golden crests highlighted above the deep shadows. As the sunlight began to fade, the colors brightened like fresh paint on an artist's canvas. If only he could take the picture home.

Think of practice as a warm-up.

Batters practice their swings before stepping up to the plate. Pitchers warm up with lots of throws before they're ready to fool the batter and hear the umpire call a strike. Try some free writing just for fun. You'll find helpful writing prompts in the Appendix.

Getting Published

*In every acceptance and rejection, give thanks in
your writing efforts, because this is God's will for
you in Christ Jesus. — 1 Thessalonians 5:18*

You may be among the millions of people who dream of writing a
bestseller. If not, maybe you should acquire that dream. As
Christians, we should believe in miracles.

God does miracles.

When the Red Sea parted, Moses saw an entire nation saved from
Pharaoh's army. What a day that must have been, but at what
cost? To get there, Moses spent eighty years of challenges, forty
years in Egypt and another forty in Midian. His experience makes
an important point: God's miracles aren't always easy. They often
come at great cost.

Only with great effort, Moses
climbed the mountain to meet God.
He got there one step at a time.
Countless others have climbed their

> Christian writers miss the
> miracle because they don't
> keep taking the next step.

mountains. No two journeys have been the same. You may not be
given two heavy stone tablets to carry, but you have a message.
Your way to your miracle is the same as for Moses: one step at a
time.

Dreams can become nightmares.

Pain and suffering is a reality of life. Without them, you
wouldn't have a story. We will all suffer for something, so we

178

might as well make the best sacrifice and write to please the Lord, not ourselves.

If you're working to satisfy your personal aspirations, get ready to survive a nightmare. Book sales won't be what you knew they should be. Your audience won't always like your message. You might be ridiculed and rejected. The only way this can be a dream fulfilled is to be content with whatever results God has for you in his plan.

If the apostle Paul were talking to writers instead of all suffering Christians, he would have said something like this:

Those who love God and keep writing their stories to fulfill his purpose should know that all their rejections will work together for good (Romans 8:28).

Success depends on giving what people want.

Agents and acquisition editors for traditional publishing houses like Tyndale and Zondervan have yet to buy a manuscript they didn't want. Of the thousands of proposals they see each year, they choose only the few that they think have the best chance of selling at least 100,000 copies.

> **Celebrity, not content or cover, usually sells the book.**

If you're a hugely popular speaker, have a large ministry drawing national attention, or have a million online followers, they might think significant profits were virtually guaranteed. In that case, the book doesn't have to be very good.

You have four main publishing choices.

Many writers aspire only to their fondest dream—to write and publish a book. They have little interest in composing effective emails, blogs, devotions, online inspirations, opinion pieces, short stories, and magazine articles. Yet those areas have the best chance of success as you improve your communication skills and grow your audience.

(1) Traditional Publishing is an unlikely option.

This is the one option that isn't really your choice. If your book proposal is so good that they can't turn down your offer, they might choose you. The odds aren't good, but it does happen.

Here's what happens in the celebrity's rise to fame:

- You have an idea for a great book.
- First-time authors must have the book written before a proposal has value.
- Develop a large audience for your book.
- Find the perfect one-sentence pitch that makes people want your book.
- Write a comprehensive book proposal that includes title, summary, back cover copy, synopsis, competing books in the genre, and first 50 pages of your manuscript.
- Find the right agent, who will find the right publisher and acquisitions editor.
- Rework your book proposal to suit each agent's submission guidelines.
- An acquisitions editor likes your book proposal, who must then convince the Publication Board to make the investment.
- The publisher offers a contract for exclusive publishing rights.
- The agent and author negotiate a final contract offer, which is accepted by all parties.
- The author's manuscript must survive substantive editing, line editing and proofing. During this time, the author may be asked to rewrite sections or chapters. Some chapters may be added and others deleted.
- Finally, production begins with the publisher's choice of book title, cover design, interior layout, typesetting, galleys, and ebook conversion. The author has limited say on the final product, because the publisher must have what it believes is best-suited for its audience.

- A marketing plan is developed, which may demand significant author time for interviews, book signings, and speaking engagements. Depending on what the publisher believes it can afford to invest, marketing may include no more than a catalog listing and little chance that the book would ever appear on a bookstore shelf.

This process will typically take between two and five years. Any cash advance is charged against royalties, which might be calculated at around 15 percent of net sales. A book at $15 retail might net at $5, with a $.75 royalty.

(2) Subsidy Publishing does all the work for you—at significant cost.

Publishing packages for your book can range from $2,500 to $10,000 and more, depending on the kind of editing, design, and marketing services being offered. Since you will be paying for more than their costs, which is essential for them to stay in business, they will have great things to say about your book's chance for success. This will boost your expectations and willingness to make the investment.

The firm is sometimes called a "vanity press" or "custom publishing." It is not an investment company under government control, compelled to say, "Past performance is no guarantee of future results." In the contract, you will read what work is promised. Sales are not guaranteed, and they assume no liability for any results. Sales and royalties earned are not guaranteed.

This process will typically take somewhere between a few months and a year. The copyright remains with the author, who has the final say on the title, cover, and content—provided all contract costs are paid and any changes and services chosen beyond the contract are also paid.

Every subsidy publisher has different provisions. A minimum author purchase of books might be required. Author cost of a $15.00 book might be at a 40 percent discount off retail, or $9.00. If a 100 percent royalty is offered, it is likely represented by the difference between $15.00 and $9.00, which is an excellent deal for the publisher, because they have no loss for books not sold and their receipts might be double their cost for books that are sold.

The chance that an author's $2,500 to $10,000 investment could be offset by sales profit is as likely as being struck by lightning on a clear day. It has happened. But the best rule to follow is: Never invest more than you can afford to lose. Whatever you choose to pay, consider it a cost of getting sales started, and never expect it to be recovered by future sales.

(3) Independent Publishing makes you the contractor.

Most homeowners buy a finished product. Only a few people are able and certified to do all the work themselves. They are the ultimate do-it-yourself builders.

Most homeowners would contact different qualified people to do the foundation, framing, electrical, plumbing, bricklaying, and drywall. This is much like what authors can do in "self-publishing" or "indie-publishing."

As a self-appointed building contractor, you might choose to do texturing, painting, or landscaping yourself and save the cost of paying someone else. As a self-published author, you decide how much help you want with writing, editing, formatting, and graphic design.

(4) Blogs let you celebrate small successes as you improve your skills and grow your audience.

No matter what your celebrity, audience, or skill level is, you should not pass up the opportunity to reach a multitude at no cost. If a blog or article doesn't grab your audience's attention, on what basis can you argue that a book on the same topic would be any better?

Finding a traditional publisher that wants your work doesn't matter as much as reaching your audience with what you have today. Write devotions, inspirational pieces, and rewarding short stories to help your audience today. Enjoy those successes now and build toward the larger work of a published book.

Or if you already have the book, excerpts and vignettes from your book will make great posts in your blog. Either way, keep working to reach more people with your rewarding stories.

If it's your book, you decide what you can afford.

You get to choose how much you will do and what you want to pay others to do. If you're homeless and have no money, you might want to nail boards and plywood under a tarp, without electricity or plumbing. Is that bad? It's certainly better than sleeping out in the cold rain or snow. If that's all you can do, it might be an important step toward finding better shelter or getting a job where you can afford more.

Technology has done wonders for the independent author. As of this writing, you can save your Microsoft Word document as a pdf file and use the free cover creator and produce a book with Kindle Direct Publishing (KDP), owned by Amazon, at zero upfront cost. The cover may look cheesy, and the content may be in bad need of rewrite and editing, but a lean-to shack of a book will still be a lot better and cheaper than paying the neighborhood copy store for printed sheets bound in a plastic cover. When you can't afford more, it's a great place to start.

KDP produces quality books at low cost.

They are so great the small traditional publishers use KDP to produce their small quantities of books at a profit. While the big publishing houses can take years to bring books to market, the small houses can use KDP and have books in your hands in a few months. Or you can do it yourself and have books in a few weeks.

Let's suppose you have a 45,000-word book totaling 180 pages, with your retail price set at $15.00. As of this writing, author copies ordered from KDP cost $3.01 each, plus shipping. Books sold on Amazon return a $5.99 royalty. If some individual should happen to order the book through a bookstore, the royalty would be $2.99.

If you are part of the 80 percent of books that don't sell 100 books in a year, here's how the costs and profits might tabulate for a $15 book:

- Traditional Publishing: two to five years requiring $0 upfront and royalties totaling $300.
- Subsidy Publishing: two months to a year requiring $2,500 upfront and royalties totaling a negative $2,200.
- Independent Publishing: two weeks requiring $0.00 upfront and royalties totaling $599. Or if the author bought copies and sold them at retail plus shipping, your profit would be $11.99 each, or $1,199.00.

Roaring Lambs Publishing offers many options.

Roaring Lambs Publishing, Frank Ball, and other associates are most concerned about helping you with whatever you need and can afford. You can learn more about this ministry at the Roaring Lambs.org, Roaring Writers.org, and FrankBall.org websites.

Success depends on expectation and effort.

If money is your mission, get ready to be disappointed. Some 80 percent of books published won't average 100 books in a year. Less than 90 percent will sell a thousand. So the success stories we read about millions sold are anomalies.

Christians have the edge when the message, not the money, is most important. In that case, quality counts more than quantity. How much is a person's life worth? If your book changes just one life, moving them to joy on Earth and a future in Heaven, the reward is priceless.

You alone can write your story.

The world isn't big enough to hold all the books that should be written about Jesus (John 21:25). Why is that true? Answer: All Christians for over 2,000 years have experienced changes in their lives that would justify at least one book—probably many more.

Whether fiction or nonfiction, fantasy or fact, your story is a unique reflection of God and his Good News.

> **Before anyone can read your story, it has to be written.**

Ask strangers if they know Jesus, and you may get the door slammed in your face. But if your stories show the problems you faced, who you were before, and how you changed, many will want to read your book.

Just write your story. That's so simple a child can do it, but not unless you're willing to invest the time and effort.

Appendix

Christianese

Don't let people despise you as a novice, but be a faith example
by seeking excellence in your writing. — *1 Timothy 4:12*

Don't assume that words we frequently hear in church will be
understood. The Christian world speaks a language that outsiders
may not understand very well.

These Christian clichés might not be clearly understood by
those who haven't yet learned the language. So here are some
ideas for what might be better words.

- Anointed — divinely gifted, empowered, or appointed
- Armor of God — God's protection
- Atonement — amends for wrongdoing
- Baptism — immersion or sprinkling to signify following Christ
- Body of Christ — people committed to following Jesus
- Born Again — motives changed to want what God wants
- Communion — celebration of Jesus' death and resurrection
- Confess — admit to wrongdoing
- Conversion — change to following God's principles
- Devotion — time to meditate upon what God wants
- Discipleship — learning to live by what God teaches
- Eschatology — study of the last days, the end of the world
- Evangelical — embracing gospel teaching and salvation through Jesus Christ
- Evangelism — telling people about Jesus

- Faith — trusting God's Word without physical evidence
- Fellowship — social networking among Christians
- Flaming Darts — accusations
- Flesh — self-serving desires
- Found the Lord — recognized the value of knowing God
- Fruit of the Spirit — doing what Jesus would do
- Get into God's Word — spend time reading the Bible
- Gospel — news of benefits of knowing Jesus
- Grace — God's unearned benevolence
- Have a Burden — deep concern for something or someone
- Heavenly Father — God in Heaven
- Hedge of Protection — keeping us safe
- Holy — set apart, uniquely special, without sin
- Holy Spirit — God's spiritual presence
- Justification — as if no wrong had been committed
- Kingdom of God — where God reigns as king
- Laid on My Heart — felt inclined
- Last Days — days preceding Jesus' promised return
- Lift Up in Prayer — speak to God on behalf of something
- Lord —Jesus as boss, leader, ruler, director
- Lost — doesn't know Jesus
- Master — Jesus as boss, leader, ruler, director
- New Birth — motives changed to want what God wants
- New Covenant — new agreement with God
- New Wine — doing what Jesus would do
- Non-Christian — someone who knows *about* Jesus but doesn't know him personally
- Offering — giving time, money, or goods to benefit a church ministry
- Old Man/New Man — old self-serving ways compared to new self-sacrificing ways of divine love
- Omnipotent — all-powerful
- Omnipresent — present everywhere

- Omniscient — knowing all things everywhere—past, present, and future
- Outreach — a church program to help others
- Praise — giving honor and thanks to God
- Prayer Warrior — someone serious about prayer
- Purity — innocent, without desire to do wrong
- Redeemed — having someone else cover our debt, obligation, or punishment
- Redeemer — Jesus, who paid the debt we could not pay
- Redemption — what was required to eliminate a debt
- Regeneration — changed, transformed, made like new
- Repentance — sorrow for wrongdoing, turning to God, and accepting forgiveness for a different life
- Reprobate — morally corrupt and unwilling to change
- Saint — a Christian fully committed to God's ways
- Salvation — forgiven for wrongdoing, free from the past to now do what is right
- Sanctification — made clean by God
- Saved — accepted God's forgiveness to follow his ways
- Savior — Jesus, who saved us from the penalty for our wrongdoing and made it possible for us to change
- Secular — society outside the Christian community
- Seeker — someone wanting to know the truth about God and his ways
- Sinners — those who fail to do the good they know they should do
- Spiritual Battle — warfare between good and evil, a fight between having our way versus surrendering to what God wants
- Spiritual Gift — God-given abilities for the fulfillment of his purpose in our lives
- Sword of the Spirit — God's Word, the Bible and its truth
- Testimony — a story about the change God has made in a person's life through Jesus Christ

- Traveling Mercies — God's protection as we walk in service to him
- Trinity — the manifestation of God in three persons: Father, Son, and Holy Spirit
- Walk with God — living according to the principles that Jesus and New Testament writers taught
- Washed in the Blood — cleansed because of Jesus' death on the cross
- Witness — share the good news about Jesus
- Worship — giving honor and thanks to God

Citing Sources

Let my concepts and writings be acceptable in your sight,
O Lord, my strength and my redeemer. — *Psalm 19:14*

Fiction storytelling has few concerns when events, names, and places must only *appear* real but aren't connected to recorded history and actual locations.

Nonfiction storytelling and historical fiction that reaches beyond your knowledge from personal experience may require listing where you got that information. Direct quotes need to cite the publication, publisher, and where the quote can be found. For nonfiction, you want credible, verifiable sources, not something you read on the internet or found in a Wikipedia article.

Record your sources while doing the research.

Don't put off for later what you can do today. Later on, you may not be able to locate a quotation source, and in that case, you can't use it.

As you find useful information, be sure to add it to your list of resources. Scan or copy a printed page or screen image and keep it in an organized file for reference. A little extra time for that now will save countless hours later.

Record the author name; title of the work; city, state, and publisher name; published date; page number; for the internet, when and where the information was accessed.

Follow the rules of your publisher, which will usually follow the practices recommended by *The Chicago Manual of Style*. For independent publishing, the following formats should be suitable.

When citing book sources:

- Bibliography: Author Last Name, First Name. *Title of the Work in Italics*. City, ST: Publisher Name, yyyy.
- Notes: Author First and Last Name, *Title of the Work in Italics* (City, ST: Publisher Name, yyyy), Page#.

When citing articles:

- Bibliography: Author Last Name, First Name. "Article Title in Quotes." *Magazine, Newspaper Name, or Internet Site in Italics*, Month dd, yyyy, Section or Page# or internet address where viewed.
- Notes: Author First and Last Name, "Article Title in Quotes," *Magazine, Newspaper Name, or Internet Site in Italics*, Month yyyy, Section or Page# or internet address where viewed.

When citing a recurrent column, show both the column title and the headline.

Give credit where credit is due.

The information you provide in your citations should make it possible for anyone to locate the source, assuming that it still exists.

Quoting Scripture

If God is our helper when we write, the stories
we build cannot be in vain. — Psalm 127:1

You may see biblical text quoted in several different ways. Here
are some examples that you might find useful:

When stating a personal conviction:

You believe your words are supported by the Bible. You aren't
making a direct quotation from any particular translation, so no
quotation marks are required. A parenthetical reference to a
particular book, chapter, and verse might be used to substantiate
your view.

- Jesus said we should love our enemies (Matthew 5:43–44).
  Are you like many Christians, sometimes finding that hard
  to do?
- Satan wanted to sift Peter like wheat. Why was that
  information relevant? Satan needed permission, and Jesus
  could have said no. Instead, Jesus prayed that Peter's faith
  would not fail (Luke 22:32).

When quoting a translation in the narrative:

On the copyright page at the front of your book, include the
information about each translation used. Google "copyright" and
the translation name, and you should be able to find the wording
required by the publisher. For example, googling "copyright

NIV" will reveal Zondervan's policies for their translations and the appropriate wording.

The letter code for the translation should appear after the reference. That code may be left out when the copyright information says the translation is used throughout unless otherwise indicated.

- Jesus said, "You should show kindness to your enemies, doing good to those who persecute you" (Matthew 5:43–44 TDB). Are you like many Christians, sometimes finding that hard to do?

- Satan wanted to sift Peter like wheat. Jesus said, "I have prayed for you, Simon, that your faith may not fail. And when you have turned back, strengthen your brothers" (Luke 22:32 NIV). Why was that information relevant? Satan needed permission, and Jesus could have said no.

Notice that the quoted text should be inside quotation marks, with the reference in parentheses after the quotation marks and the period placed after that. No period should be inside the closing quotation marks.

When words are left out:

Show the book, chapter, and verse numbers where the quoted text can be found.

Readers know you are quoting a portion of biblical text, so you don't need to indicate the front or ending portion of a verse with an *a* or *b* after the reference. It's not necessary to show an ellipsis at the beginning or the end to show left-out words. When beginning or ending words are omitted, capitalize the first word and end with a period. When interior words are left out, either use an ellipsis to show the left-out words or include condensed representative words in square brackets.

"If I speak with human excellence and angelic might yet don't really care for the wellbeing of those I serve, my message is like a noisy gong or clanging cymbal, getting attention but not really helping" (1 Corinthians 13:1 TDB).

- "If I . . . don't really care for the wellbeing of those I serve, my message is like a noisy gong or clanging cymbal" (1 Corinthians 13:1 TDB).

"In the past God spoke to our ancestors through the prophets at many times and in various ways, but in these last days he has spoken to us by his Son, whom he appointed heir of all things, and through whom also he made the universe" (Hebrews 1:1–2 NIV).

- "God spoke to our ancestors through the prophets at many times and in various ways, but [now] he has spoken to us by his Son . . . through whom also he made the universe" (Hebrews 1:1–2 NIV).

Verses can be set after bullet points.

Set apart like this, quote marks and parentheses aren't required. Let the reference follow an em-dash.

- If I . . . don't really care for the wellbeing of those I serve, my message is like a noisy gong or clanging cymbal. — 1 Corinthians 13:1 TDB
- God spoke to our ancestors through the prophets at many times and in various ways, but [now] he has spoken to us by his Son . . . through whom also he made the universe. — Hebrews 1:1–2 NIV

Italics might be used to distinguish Scripture.

As part of chapter headings, you might want to make a biblical reference like this, using italics instead of quotes.

Athletes give their lives in strenuous training for a short-lived glory, but writers strive for a reward that will last forever. — 1 Corinthians 9:25

Contranyms

The words of deceivers shed innocent blood, but
godly writing saves lives. — Proverbs 12:6

Nothing illustrates the importance of context more than an English word that can have opposite meanings.

- All Over: available everywhere / no longer available
- Anxious: eager expectation / fearful apprehension
- Apart: separated / included (a part)
- Apology: statement of contrition / statement of defense
- Argue: assert / deny
- Awful: awe-inspiring / terribly bad
- Bad: terrible / wonderfully good
- Bill: money held ($5 bill) / money owed
- Bolt: hold securely / run away
- Bound: moving / unable to move
- Buckle: hold together / collapse or fall apart
- Carry On: behave normally / behave abnormally
- Cleave: cut apart / join together
- Clip: fasten / detach
- Consult: give advice / ask for advice
- Citation: award for good behavior / penalty for bad behavior
- Clip: attach to / cut off from
- Custom: common practice / special treatment

Contranyms

- Cut: get into (a line) / get out of (a class)
- Downhill: a better direction / a worse direction
- Dress: add a covering (clothes)/ remove a covering (plucked feathers)
- Dust: remove fine particles / cover with fine particles
- Enjoin: prescribe / prohibit
- Execute: kill / implement, bringing it to life
- Fast: moving rapidly / holding a fixed position
- Fight with: join in battle / oppose in battle
- Finished: completed / destroyed
- First degree: most severe (murder) / least severe (burns)
- Fix: predicament / solution
- Garnish: enhance (food) / take away (wages)
- Go off: begin operation / cease operation
- Grade: incline / level
- Hold up: support / impede
- Impregnable: not enterable / enterable
- Lease: buy use of / sell use of
- Left: remaining / gone away
- Legendary: famously true / famously imaginary
- Mirror Image: exactly the same / exactly the opposite
- Moot: arguable / not worthy of an argument
- Oblige: require a favor / do a favor
- Out: visible (stars) / invisible (lights)
- Oversight: watchful control / something not noticed
- Peer: unequal (nobility to a peasant) / an equal
- Pitted: with pits / with pits removed
- Put out: extinguish / initiate
- Rent: buy use of / sell use of
- Resign: quit / continue
- Sanction: approve / forbid (boycott)
- Scan: carefully inspect / skim over

- Screen: make visible (as a movie) / hide from view
- Seeded: with seeds / with seeds removed
- Shelled: having a shell / having no shell
- Skinned: with the skin on / with the skin removed
- Splice: join / separate
- Strike: hit (oil) / fail to hit (baseball)
- Submit: offer / accept
- Table: bring up for discussion / withdraw from discussion
- Temper: soften / strengthen
- Throw out: disregard / consider
- Transparent: invisible / obvious
- Trim: add (decorations) / remove (excess)
- Variety: particular type / many types
- Wear: endure / deteriorate
- Weather: withstand the elements / worn away by the elements
- Wind up: end / start up

Expressions, Posture, and Actions

Commit your writing to the Lord, and your message will touch people's hearts. — Proverbs 16:3

When she is angry, how does she look? What does she do? The volume and pitch of her voice rises. She could raise her fist or stomp out of the room. When you have trouble drawing a word picture of your character's emotion, the following descriptions of typical body language and actions might help.

- Aggression: eyes intense, hands on hips, pointing the finger, aiming a hand in the form of a gun, raised fist, finger poked in someone's chest, a push, finger drawn across the throat like a knife, sitting on someone's desk, leaning into someone's space, raised voice
- Anger: clenched lips, flared nostrils, glaring eyes blinking less than normal, reddened face, furrowed brow, raised voice, slammed fist, sudden change in position, thrown objects, stomped foot, voice is high pitch and volume, spoken at a fast rate, brow lowered, eyebrows lowered and drawn together, clenched fist, tightened jaw, lips tightened and turned downward, smile is forced, hands on hips
- Anxiety: furrowed brow, tense cheeks, trembling lips, raised eyebrows drawn together, raised eyelids, showing whites of the eyes, quivering stomach, chest tightness
- Approval, attentive: body leaning forward, eyes in constant contact, head nodding, lips with a genuine smile, open palms
- Bad Smell: pinched nose, head turned away

- Blame Accepted: open hands pulled inward, pointing at one's chest
- Bored, Closed Mind: crossing legs, leaning back, arms closed across the chest, looking elsewhere, lowered head, finger drumming, foot tapping, picking imaginary lint from clothing, hands in pockets, smug lips, yawning
- Concentrating: furrowed brow, focused eyes, stroking the chin, hand touches or rubs the lips, hand scratches the head
- Confident: arms locked across the chest, hands clasped behind the head, measured pace, walking erect, chin high, head and hands move in a hair toss, lips give an occasional, genuine smile with crow's-feet crinkle outside the eyes, arms relaxed at ones side, body leaning forward, steady eye contact, hands clasped behind back, erect posture
- Confusion: shrug with outstretched arms and open palms, hesitation, averting the eyes, lips raised in a sneer, lips tighten, wrinkling the nose, voice is low pitch and volume, spoken at a slow rate, clearing the throat
- Controlling: finger pointing, hand makes a chopping motion onto the other hand, palms turn forward as if pushing away, body pushes forward, invading personal space, hands on hips, folded arms, intense eyes
- Deception: averting the eyes, turning head to the side, scratching back of neck, stroking the chin, faked cough, lips in a frequent, rubbing the nose, faked smile with no crinkle outside the eyes, short and incomplete responses, vague answers with few details, sweating, swallowing
- Disappointment: sighing, averted eyes, grimace, blank stare, forced smile, quiet
- Disapproval: body leaning back, eyes looking away, fingers drumming, head shaking, folded arms, averted eyes, lips in a smirk
- Disbelief: wide eyes, tight lips, raised eyebrows
- Disgust: wrinkled nose, raised cheeks, lowered brow, averted eyes, lips narrow with a frown, lips tightened in a

scowl, stiffened chin, voice is low pitch and volume, spoken at a slow rate

- Dread: furrowed brow, tense cheeks, trembling lips, raised eyebrows drawn together, raised eyelids, showing whites of the eyes, shifting weight from one foot to the other, eyes blink more than normal, licking lips, shrugging
- Eager: eyes intense, hands on hips, pointing the finger, aiming a hand in the form of a gun, raised fist, finger poked in someone's chest, a push, finger drawn across the throat like a knife, sitting on someone's desk, leaning into someone's space, raised voice
- Embarrassed: biting lips, face reddens, speechless
- Excited: faster pulse rate, voice raised in pitch, fast talking, can't sit still
- Fearful: furrowed brow, tense cheeks, trembling lips, raised eyebrows drawn together, raised eyelids, showing whites of the eyes, shifting weight from one foot to the other, eyes blink more than normal, licking lips, shrugging
- Forgetting: slap on the forehead, a raised finger, scratching the chin
- Frustration: tense cheeks, trembling lips, raised eyebrows drawn together, raised eyelids, showing whites of the eyes, pacing, eyes blink more than normal, licking lips, shrugging
- Good News: thumb raised, fist thrust forward and down, slapping someone's open palm
- Gratitude: a kiss, shaking hands, pat on the back, applause
- Guilt: tears down the cheeks, subdued frown, dropped chin, eyes staring downward, silence, crying, choking on words, resting head in hands, voice is low pitch and volume, spoken at a slow rate
- Happy: smile, adding wrinkles outside the eyes, exposed teeth, bright eyes, sparkle in the eyes, chronic genuine smile, voice is high pitch and volume, spoken at a fast rate, light-footed, dancing

- Hatred: clenched lips, flared nostrils, glaring eyes blinking less than normal, reddened face, furrowed brow, raised voice, slammed fist, sudden change in position, thrown objects, stomped foot, voice is high pitch and volume, spoken at a fast rate, brow lowered, eyebrows lowered and drawn together, clenched fist, tightened jaw, lips tightened and turned downward, smile is forced, hands on hips
- Honest: holds steady eye contact, hand motions with open palms, lips acquire a slow, genuine smile
- Hopeful: smile, adding wrinkles outside the eyes, exposed teeth, bright eyes, sparkle in the eyes, chronic genuine smile, voice is high pitch and volume, spoken at a fast rate
- Impatient: eyes toward the clock or the door, rubbing hands, finger drumming, foot tapping, pacing
- Insecure: touching the mouth while speaking, brushing hair with fingers, biting fingernails, tapping fingers or other unconscious repetitive movements, trembling voice, rapid clearing of throat, sweating, weak voice
- Intolerant: hand playing an imaginary violin
- Listening: tilted head, on the edge of the seat, leaning forward, arms separated, cupping a hand behind the ear
- Lying: averting the eyes, turning head to the side, scratching back of neck, stroking the chin, faked cough, lips in a frequent, rubbing the nose, faked smile with no crinkle outside the eyes, short and incomplete responses, vague answers with few details, sweating, swallowing
- Money Needed: rubbing thumb against fingers
- Nervous: touching the mouth while speaking, brushing hair with fingers, biting fingernails, tapping fingers or other unconscious repetitive movements, trembling voice, rapid clearing of throat, sweating, weak voice, swaying body, jingling car keys, averting eyes, drumming fingers, chewing fingernails, tapping feet, chewing on something, lips show a rare, faked smile

- Pain: touching the stomach or some place that hurts, real or imaginary
- Puzzled: wrinkled brow, straight lips
- Recognition: body leans forward, eyebrows rise, eyes hold contact, head nods
- Relief: hand wiped across the brow
- Resignation: stepping back, bowed head, turning away, hands in the pockets, silence, shrugging
- Sadness: furrowed brow, droopy eyelids, watery eyes, tears down the cheeks, subdued frown, dropped chin, eyes staring downward, silence, crying, choking on words, resting head in hands, voice is low pitch and volume, spoken at a slow rate
- Sexual Interest: moving closer, eyes make contact longer than normal, shift away, then back, smoothing one's clothing, tossing the hair, head tilts in a sideways glance, shoulders push back, legs cross and uncross
- Shame: tears down the cheeks, subdued frown, dropped chin, eyes staring downward, silence, crying, choking on words, resting head in hands, voice is low pitch and volume, spoken at a slow rate
- Shock: stone-faced, blank stare, glassy eyes, raised eyebrows
- Sincerity: hand over the heart
- Stupid: rotating finger pointed at one's temple, slapping the forehead, slapping the side of the head
- Superiority: raising the chin, steepling the fingers, placing hands on hips, looking down the nose, lips show a condescending smirk, shaking the head in denying respect of others
- Surprise: raised eyebrows, wide eyes, dropped jaw, open mouth, hint of a smile, voice is high pitch and volume, words spoken at a rising rate
- Thinking: hesitation or pause, scratching the scalp, rubbing the chin, walking with hands clasped behind the back, closed eyes, resting chin on hand

- Trustworthy: steady eye contact, submissive shrugs, tilted head, lips give a slow and genuine smile, hand gestures are made with palms up, sits and stands tall and straight
- Uncomfortable: squirming, repetitive movements
- Yes: thumb raised, fist thrust forward and down, slapping someone's open palm

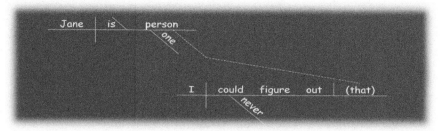

Prepositional Verbs

Write your message in an article or a book so it
may be an everlasting witness. — Isaiah 30:8

The old claim that one should never end a sentence with a preposition is wrong.

Here are some examples:

- back off — If he knows what's good for him, he'll back off.
- be in — What a pickle he must be in.
- bend over — Bend over and take your punishment.
- black out — Not moving, he appears to have blacked out.
- break down — Tim's car broke down.
- break up — Why did Jack and Jill break up?
- bring up — Why did you have to bring that up?
- burst in — Frantic with the news, she burst in.
- call in — Did Bill call in?
- call off — Has the search been called off?
- calm down — Johnnie just needs to calm down.
- charge with — Do you know what he's been charged with?
- check in — Is it too early to check in?
- come down — It's about time he came down to earth.
- count on — Are you someone we can count on?
- deal with — What are we dealing with?
- do without — Eating isn't something we can do without.
- drop by — Did Jason say when he would drop by?

207

- fence in — Don't fence me in.
- figure out — Jane is one person I could never figure out.
- get by — He makes barely enough to get by.
- get up — How early did you get up?
- go in — I believe we can now go in.
- go through — The email wouldn't go through.
- hang out — This is a comfortable place to hang out.
- hang up — In mid-conversation, it's rude to hang up.
- hurry up — Will you please hurry up?
- mess with — He's not someone you should mess with.
- pass away — Both her parents have passed away.
- pass out — Hold your breath very long, and you'll pass out.
- put on — He put his shoes on, without socks.
- replace with — There's nothing to replace it with.
- rule out — The possibility cannot be ruled out.
- run away — Did her teenage daughter run away?
- see through — Transparency means you can see through.
- set up — Is the room set up?
- show off — Jimmy, why do you have to show off?
- shut down — The equipment was shut down.
- sign in — Don't forget to sign in.
- sleep in — Did the kids let you sleep in?
- slow down — A cop would tell you to slow down.
- sober up — Coffee will help you sober up.
- speak up — For me to understand, you'll have to speak up.
- spread out — The coach told his players to spread out.
- stand around — You'll be in trouble if you stand around.
- stand by — For an important message, please stand by.
- start over — Did the teacher say we had to start over?
- step aside — Will you please step aside?
- stop by — If you want to see me perform, please stop by.
- straighten out — Is this mess something to straighten out?

- throw up — The drunk leaned forward and threw up.
- turn off — The television needs to be turned off.
- wake up — Johnnie, it's time to wake up.
- walk away — Without saying a word, they walked away.
- work with — She's a hard person to work with.

Redundant Words

While waiting for the Lord, write. Be strong and take heart, and keep writing for the Lord. — Psalm 27:14

We might think redundant words add emphasis, and in some teaching situations, that's true. But for storytelling, redundancy is a distraction. Although we hear them in newscasts and in everyday speech, we should avoid them in our writing.

In the following phrases, the word in parentheses can be left out.

- (absolutely) necessary
- (across) to the other side
- (actual) facts
- (advance) planning
- (advance) reservations
- (advance) warning
- add (an additional)
- add (more)
- add (up)
- (added) bonus
- (adolescent) boy
- (all-time) record
- alternative (choice)
- a.m. (in the morning)
- (anonymous) stranger

- (armed) gunman
- ascend (up)
- ask (the question)
- assemble (together)
- attach (together)
- ATM (machine)
- autobiography (of his life)
- bald (headed)
- balsa (wood)
- (basic) fundamentals
- (basic) necessities
- best (ever)
- biography (of his life)
- blend (together)

- bouquet (of flowers)
- brief (duration)
- (brief) moment
- (brief) summary
- (burning) embers
- cancel (out)
- (careful) scrutiny
- cascading (down)
- cash (money)
- cease (and desist)
- circle (around)
- classify (into groups)
- (close) proximity
- (closed) fist
- clutching (in her hands)
- collaborate (together)
- combine (together)
- commute (back and forth)
- compete (with one another)
- (completely) annihilate
- (completely) destroy
- (completely) eliminate
- (completely) engulf
- (completely) fill
- (completely) surround
- (component) part
- connect (together)
- connect (up)
- consensus (of opinion)
- (constantly) maintained
- cooperate (together)

- could (possibly)
- crisis (situation)
- (current) trend
- (deliberately) choose
- depreciate (in value)
- descend (down)
- (desirable) benefit
- (different) kinds
- disappear (from sight)
- drop (down)
- (dry) parched
- during (the course of)
- dwindle (down)
- each (and every)
- earlier (in time)
- eliminate (altogether)
- emergency (situation)
- (empty) hole
- (end) result
- enter (in)
- (entirely) eliminate
- equal (to each another)
- eradicate (completely)
- estimated at (about)
- evolve (over time)
- (exact) same
- (exposed) opening
- fall (down)
- (favorable) approval
- (fellow) associates
- (fellow) classmates
- few (in number)

- filled (to capacity)
- (final) conclusion
- (final) outcome
- (first and) foremost
- (first) conceived
- first (of all)
- fly (through the air)
- follow (after)
- (foreign) imports
- (former) graduate
- (former) veteran
- (free) gift
- (frozen) ice
- full (to capacity)
- (fully) satisfied
- fuse (together)
- (future) plans
- (future) recurrence
- gather (together)
- (general) public
- grow (in size)
- had done (previously)
- (harmful) injuries
- (head) honcho
- heat (up)
- heave (up)
- HIV (virus)
- hoist (up)
- (hollow) tube
- hope (for the future)
- hurry (up)
- (illustrated) drawing
- incredible (to believe)
- indicted (on a charge)
- integrate (together)
- introduced (a new)
- introduced (for the first time)
- join (together)
- (joint) collaboration
- kneel (down)
- (knowledgeable) experts
- lag (behind)
- later (time)
- lift (up)
- (little) baby
- (live) studio audience
- (live) witness
- (local) resident
- look (on her face)
- look (ahead) to the future
- look back (in retrospect)
- looked (over)
- made (out) of
- (major) breakthrough
- (major) feat
- manually (by hand)
- marina (on the lake)
- may (possibly)
- meet (together)
- meet (with each other)
- (mental) telepathy
- merge (together)
- might (possibly)

- mix (together)
- (mutual) cooperation
- mutual respect (for each other)
- nape (of his neck)
- (native) habitat
- (natural) instinct
- never (before)
- (new) beginning
- (new) construction
- (new) innovation
- (new) invention
- (new) recruit
- nodded (in approval)
- none (at all)
- off (of)
- (old) adage
- (old) cliché
- (old) custom
- (old) proverb
- (open) trench
- open (up)
- (oral) conversation
- (originally) created
- outcome (as a result)
- output (out of)
- (outside) in the yard
- outside (of)
- (over) exaggerate
- (pair of) twins
- palm (of his hand)
- (passing) fad

- (past) experience
- (past) history
- (past) memories
- (past) records
- penetrate (into)
- period (of time)
- (personal) friend
- (personal) opinion
- pick (and choose)
- plan (ahead)
- plan (in advance)
- (Please) RSVP
- plunge (down)
- (polar) opposite
- (positive) identification
- postpone (until later)
- pouring (down) rain
- (present) incumbent
- present (time)
- previously listed (above)
- proceed (ahead)
- protest (against)
- pursue (after)
- raise (up)
- reason (why)
- recur (again)
- refer (back)
- reflect (back)
- (regular) routine
- repeat (again)
- reply (back)
- revert (back)

- (right) behind
- rise (up)
- round (in shape)
- (safe) haven
- (safe) sanctuary
- same (exact)
- scrutinize (in detail)
- (serious) danger
- setting sun (in the west)
- share (together)
- (sharp) point
- shiny (in appearance)
- shrugged (his shoulders)
- shut (down)
- skipped (over)
- slow (speed)
- small (size)
- (small) speck
- soft (to the touch)
- sole (of the foot)
- (specific) things
- spell out (in detail)
- spliced (together)
- start (out)
- (still) persists
- (still) remains
- stuffed (full)
- (sudden) impulse
- (sum) total
- surrounded (on all sides)
- tall (in height)
- tall (in stature)

- (temper) tantrum
- ten (in number)
- (three-way) love triangle
- time (period)
- (tiny) bit
- (total) destruction
- (true) facts
- (truly) sincere
- (twelve) noon
- (two equal) halves
- (ultimate) goal
- (underground) subway
- (unexpected) emergency
- (unexpected) surprise
- (unintentional) mistake
- (universal) panacea
- (unknown) stranger
- (usual) custom
- vacillate (back and forth)
- (veiled) ambush
- (very) pregnant
- (very) unique
- visible (to the eye)
- (visually) inspected
- mural (on the wall)
- warn (in advance)
- weather (conditions)
- weather (situation)
- whether (or not)
- (white) snow
- write (down)

Shades of Meaning

The Lord is good, a wonderful retreat when we
suffer from writer's block. He recognizes those
who seek him for guidance. — Nahum 1:7

Many words sound alike or have similar applications, which can be confusing. Besides the *right* word, we need the *best* word for what we want to say.

A or The

We use *a* in generalization, *the* when referring to a specific object.

The boy climbs *a* tree when it has no particular distinction from any other, but he is more likely to climb *the* big oak in his back yard because of its low branches.

Accept or Except

Accept is to take something given to you. *Except* is to exclude something.

Except for one detail, the office could *accept* the man's story.

Aggravate or Annoy

Aggravate means to worsen or intensify. *Annoy* means to disturb or bother someone.

People may be *annoyed* by the *aggravated* air quality.

Affect or Effect

Affect is a verb meaning "to have an influence upon." *Effect* is a noun referring to a resulting change.

A negative *effect* occurs when we *affect* people in the wrong way.

Allusion or Illusion

An *allusion* refers to something in an indirect way. Seeing what isn't really there is an *illusion*.

An *allusion* to Darwin's theory doesn't keep evolution from being an *illusion*.

Alright or All Right

Alright fought to be a one-word spelling for *all right* for many years, but it has lost that war. Editors generally hold to the exclusive use of *all right*. So in *all ways*, we *always* use *all right* in the two-word form.

But you might consider an exception. In the rare case where *all right* is used as an adjective, you might be accepted as an *alright* person to use the single word. In dialog, we might hear someone say, "*Alright* now, let's quit quibbling over quibbles."

Alternatives or Options

Both words have to do with choice, but the perspective is slightly different. An *alternative* says you have one choice other than what is most preferred. *Options* suggest any number of choices of somewhat equal value.

After ruling out several *options*, Bill had only one *alternative* to his first choice.

Among or Between

These two prepositions have an important distinction in meaning. Both refer to a relevant position of something. *Among* refers to a relationship to three or more people, places, or things. *Between* defines a position in relation to exactly two.

Among several scholarship offers, Caleb had to choose *between* Notre Dame and Princeton.

Anxious or Eager

Anxious is associated with *anxiety*, referring to apprehension, a negative emotion, which is often confused with someone who is *eager*, a positive emotion of anticipation. To avoid confusion when the context doesn't make the meaning clear, use *fearful* or *apprehensive* instead of *anxious*.

Fred was *anxious* about sky jumping for the first time but afterward was *eager* to go again.

Ascent or Assent

Ascent is an upward climb. *Assent* means to agree or approve. The *ascent* was too steep for the guide to give his *assent*.

At or In

At marks a location or the start of something happening.

In refers to a container where, or a time when, something exists or happens.

He lived *at* home. The train left *at* 6:42 p.m. They stopped *at* the corner café. He was dressed *in* his tuxedo. They played *in* the afternoon.

At the beginning, he wrote what happened *in* the beginning.

Awhile or A While

Awhile is a noun referring to a period of time. After a preposition, a noun by itself makes no sense. We need an article *a*, *an*, or *the* preceding *while*. For example, we wouldn't say, "For house," but rather, "For *the* house." Following the same principle, we don't want to say, "For awhile," but rather, "For a while," using the two-word form after the preposition.

Give John *awhile* to make up his mind, and after *a while* we'll have his decision.

Belief or Faith

For many people, "faith" and "belief" are two words for the same thing. However, we can make a distinction that might be important. *Belief* is something that is accepted as true and held as an opinion, perhaps because we want it to be true. *Faith* is an

217

unwavering conviction of a truth, especially when we trust God's Word above physical evidence.

Abraham held a *belief* in God, and when he trusted God's promise as absolute truth, he had *faith*.

Jason listed his *beliefs* in God and Jesus Christ as "Statements of *Faith*" because he held each one to be absolutely true.

Capital or Capitol

Capital might be money to start a business, something of chief importance, or a center for government. *Capitol* is the building where the government meets.

More *capital* was needed to started a business in the state's *capital* city near the *capitol*.

Cite, Sight, or Site

Cite means to quote or call attention to something. *Sight* is the ability to see or something seen. *Site* is a place where something is located.

At this *site*, the *sight* was too breathtaking for him to *cite* any place that was more beautiful.

Complement or Compliment

Complement means to combine well with something else. A *compliment* is saying something nice, praising someone.

She received a *compliment* because her spicy casserole was the perfect *complement* for the rest of the meal.

Conscious or Conscience

Conscious people are awake and aware of their surroundings. *Conscience* refers to the feeling we have when doing right or wrong.

Conscious that nobody was looking, his *conscience* still would not allow him to steal.

Continually or Continuously

The two words might seem interchangeable, because both refer to something ongoing. But there is an important distinction.

Continually describes a frequent occurrence that might be interrupted. *Continuously* allows no interruption.

To satisfy his occasional boredom, John *continually* picked up a box of dominoes and *continuously* placed each one on end so the first to fall would take all the rest down.

Counsel or Council

Counsel is to give advice or be one who gives advice. A *council* is a group of people chosen to make decisions or give advice.

Lacking important information, the *council* was not able to provide *counsel* on the issue.

Crucial or Critical

While the two might be used interchangeably, *critical* works best for extreme danger and *crucial* for something very important.

It may be *crucial* to pay bills on time, but when the debtor is about to be sued, his condition has become *critical*.

Day Before or Yesterday

The correct word and meaning depend on the point of view. *Yesterday* refers to the *day before* the present day in the story. The *day before* refers to whatever day precedes the current day in focus, which could be any day, even in the future.

Yesterday, I didn't know as much as I know today, which is the *day before* tomorrow.

Eldest or Oldest

Both *eldest* and *oldest* refer to age, but a distinction does exist. *Eldest* refers only to people in relation to two or more other people. If the comparison is with only one person, *elder*, is correct, although common practice seems to prefer use of *older* and *oldest*, which can work for age comparison of anything, including people.

Jim is the *eldest* sibling, who drives the *oldest* car, and Jane is the *elder* of the two sisters.

Elicit or Illicit

Elicit means to get information or cause a desired reaction. *Illicit* is something unacceptable or unlawful.

He didn't mean to *elicit* an *illicit* response.

End or Ending

In conversation, people might use *end* and *ending* interchangeably, but you can probably sense a slight difference in meaning. *End* marks a point of conclusion with zero duration. The *ending* can be much longer. For example: The *end* of a book might be regarded as the last words on the last page, which said, "The End." But the *ending* would be what comes after the climax, the last chapter, perhaps.

The *end* of a race is the finish line. The *ending* is that last sprint to achieve the best time.

Euphemism or Pretense

A *euphemism* is a substitute word or phrase for what might be otherwise regarded as unpleasant. A *pretense* represents something as other than what it really is. Instead of saying the mayor had died, reporters used *euphemisms*, saying, "He passed away," "He departed this life," or "He went to Heaven."

He excused himself from the business meeting under the *pretense* that he had to make an important call.

Exalt / Exaltation or Exult / Exultation

Since these words are often used interchangeably, your dictionary might offer little distinction, but there is one. *Exaltation* is best defined as the glorification or elevation of a person or thing. *Exultation* focuses on the feeling we have, our being so filled with joy that the overflow must be expressed.

We should *exalt* the Lord Jesus for all he has done for us and have *exultation* for the indescribable peace and joy we feel.

Famous or Notorious

Famous people are known for their achievements, their position in society. *Notorious* people are known for their wrongdoing, their criminal activities.

Roy Rogers is a *famous* cowboy, and Jesse James is a *notorious* criminal.

Farther or Further

Farther refers to physical distance, which is easy to remember if you notice that the word contains "far." *Further* applies to distance in the metaphorical or figurative sense.

If we need to drive *farther* down the road, we'll need *further* instruction.

Flier or Flyer

The debate continues. When referring to a pilot or a handbill, which word is correct? Some say it doesn't matter. Others want "flyer" for both. If the pundits can't agree, we should consider the most likely reader perception.

A pilot is much different from a handbill, so distinct words would be useful. Since "flyer" contains "fly," which is what pilots do, let's use "flyer" for pilots and airplane passengers. Use "flier" for handbills. Few people will complain if you use "flyer" for both, but avoid using "flier" for pilots.

The stewardess gave printed *fliers* to all the frequent *flyers*.

Healthy or Healthful

Use *healthful* when the intended meaning is "promoting good health." *Healthy* applies to anything in good health.

A *healthful* snack will keep us *healthy*.

Hearing or Listening

In conversation, the meanings of the two words are sometimes confused, but an important distinction exists. *Hearing* is the ability to perceive sound. *Listening* is a conscious choice that requires mental focus.

Grandpa isn't hard of *hearing*, but when his mind wanders, he isn't *listening*.

Here or There

The difference is in whether we see the object as close or distant.

Here we have something either in my hand or close, but over *there* we have something that is more distant.

Historic or Historical

Historic refers to something especially worth noting in history. *Historical* simply identifies something from the past.

Neil Armstrong's first step on lunar soil was an *historic* event, and the museum contains many *historical* items from the first decades of space travel.

Honorarium or Compensation

An *honorarium* is a reward of an unspecified nature or amount. *Compensation* is payment of an agreed-upon fee.

The speaker anticipated an *honorarium* of a gift card or cash because he had no agreement for any *compensation*.

Immanent or Imminent

Something *immanent* exists everywhere. Something *imminent* is likely or certain to happen very soon.

Fear is *immanent* in human nature when arrival of a hurricane is *imminent*.

Instance or Instant

An *instance* is an occurrence, a moment in time. *Instant* refers to something sudden or quick, marking the speed of time. After three *instances* of failure, he was looking for *instant* success. A *moment* can be an *instance*, but not an *instant*.

For an insane *instant*, she longed for an *instance* when he would kiss her.

Ironic or Unusual

Anything that deviates from the norm, from what would be expected, is *unusual*. Something is *ironic* when the meaning is in direct contrast, opposite to what would be expected.

The nickname Tater Tot is *ironic* when it refers to a lineman playing in the NFL, and his never playing college ball would be *unusual*.

Its or It's

Because possessives are so often formed by adding apostrophe-s, using *it's* as a possessive pronoun is an understandable mistake. The word *it's* is a contraction for "it is," and *its* is the possessive pronoun.

It's true that a leopard cannot change *its* spots.

Lead or Led

As a noun, *lead* refers to the front or superior position. As a verb, *lead* is a present action that takes followers in a certain direction. *Led* is a verb describing a past action that took followers in a certain direction.

Loving to *lead* people to success, the teacher took the *lead* and *led* his students through the manual.

Lie or Lay

Confusion comes in the way the verbs are used in different tenses.

(1) The verb *lie* means to tell something that isn't true. Jack is *lying*. He *lies* now, *lied* yesterday, and *has lied* more times than one can count.

(2) Or *lie* means to be at rest. Jack *lies* now, *lay* yesterday, and *has lain* when tired.

(3) *Lay* means to put or place something. If a chicken yields an egg, it *lays* now, *laid* yesterday, and *has laid* an egg almost every day. When the grammatically correct verb form doesn't match what is common in everyday speech, find a different word so readers won't mistakenly think you wrote incorrectly.

Loose or Lose

Something *loose* does not fit tightly, isn't securely fastened, or is free from constraint. *Lose* is failure to keep something or falling short of winning.

Loose living is an easy way to *lose* a good reputation.

Naked or Nude

Nude refers to a person wearing no clothes, and only rarely might be used as a metaphor, such as *nude furniture*, referring to unfinished wood. The meaning of *naked* can go much further than being unclothed, meaning *stripped down, vulnerable, unprotected*. Artists learn to paint *nudes*, and that's the *naked truth*.

Near or Close

Think of *close* as referring to something intimate, *near* as something positioned a little farther away. We might have a *close* call, a *close* friend, or a *close* encounter of the third kind. In the *near* future, we might move to a neighborhood *near* the big city.

Negligent or Negligible

Negligent describes chronic ignoring or overlooking responsibilities. *Negligible* is something too insignificant to warrant any concern. Because Jack was *negligent* in reporting the accident, he was fired. A two-cent difference in the cost for a gallon of gas is *negligible*.

Passed or Past

Passed refers to movement from one place or condition to another. *Past* is the time before the present or points to a place farther down the road.

He walked *past* the school, *passed* the playground, and recalled *past* pleasures.

Precede or Proceed

To *precede* means to come before something. To *proceed* means to make progress, to go in a particular direction.

If preparation *precedes* the journey, they can *proceed* with confidence.

Principle or Principal

Principle refers to a basic belief, rule, or standard. *Principal* refers to the main or most important thing, an original monetary amount, or the main person in an organization.

The *principal* message by the school *principal* presented the *principle* that all are created equal.

Shall or Will

While these words are often understood as identical twins, *shall* has a stronger feeling of intent, with a sense of command, and *will* is more common in everyday speech, more casual and less formal. I *shall* not lie, but I *will* probably shade the truth a bit. When in doubt, use the contraction: I think *I'll* stay home.

Stationary or Stationery

Something *stationary* is not moving and might be impossible to move. *Stationery* refers to paper and other materials used in writing.

A *stationary* printer needs *stationery* to produce copies.

There, They're, or Their

There introduces a statement or refers to a place where something is located. *They're* is a contraction for "they are." *Their* is a possessive pronoun, meaning belonging to someone.

There are times when *they're* going to miss *their* friends.

These or Those

The difference is in how you see the condition.

These marbles are much closer to me than *those* marbles.

This or That

The difference is in how close the items are.

This hailstone, the one I'm holding in my hand, is larger than *that* one over there.

Think or Believe

Think refers to an idea or concept, our rational and objective evaluation of something that is possibly or probably true. *Believe* refers to what we hold as absolutely true.

We might *think* we can use these words interchangeably, but *believing* we can shows a deep conviction.

To, Too, or Two

To is a preposition introducing a phrase. *Too* means "also." And *two* is the whole number between one and three.

To convict a criminal, having the agreement of *two* eyewitnesses would be good *too*.

Throwaway Words

Oh that my words were written with an iron pen on a granite tablet so my story could be read forever. — Job 19:23–24

When words don't add meaning, they should be thrown away, strengthening what remains. The words below are worthy of inspection to determine whether they are ~~really~~ necessary.

- Able to — Catherine ~~was able to~~ (saw) trouble coming.
- All — When do ~~all~~ the members get an invitation?
- Always/Never — People should ~~always~~ watch their diets.
- Any — Johnny didn't want ~~any~~ help.
- Essentially — The product is ~~essentially~~ of no use.
- Just — She ~~just~~ didn't know what to do.
- Literally — He was ~~literally~~ knocked to the ground.
- Of the — Most ~~of the~~ students failed the exam.
- Own — Should I go my ~~own~~ way or God's way?
- Particular — What do you know about this ~~particular~~ situation?
- Really — If a word isn't needed, we ~~really~~ should throw it away.
- Some — I've been having ~~some~~ doubts.
- Somehow — Can we ~~somehow~~ reduce the number of words?
- Successfully — They ~~successfully~~ completed the assignment.
- That — I know ~~that~~ we don't have time to get ready.

- Then — He looked up and ~~then~~ saw something amazing.
- Totally — The employees were ~~totally~~ committed to making the plan work.
- Very — This is a ~~very~~ crucial meeting.

Writing Prompts

*Beyond fantasies and wishful thinking, let writers publish
stories that let readers experience truth.* — *Jeremiah 23:28*

Great stories present a problem in which readers eagerly follow
the character's emotional journey to find out what happens. The
problem and solution are the "bookends" for the pages in
between, which show how the character is changed by the
experience.

With one of the following prompts, can you think of a
problem worth writing about?

- My best friend became an enemy when…
- I used to love playing _____ until…
- When people called me _____, I laughed but wanted
  to…
- Every time I see a freeway accident, I remember the time
  when…
- I was doing well at school, but then…
- If I could escape from _____, I would be…
- My pasted-on smile wasn't enough to fool my…
- I could not have been more surprised when…
- After I lost my _____, I decided to…
- On my birthday, I was given…
- I've tried many things, but I never thought I'd…
- If I could do it over again, I would…
- I thought I had been dreaming, but then…

- When I was a kid, I most liked to…
- From the moment Dad told me I had to _____, I wanted to…
- If I took just one more step, I felt sure I would…
- After I overslept, I was faced with…
- When I had to dress up like _____, I…
- The day was so hot, I just had to…
- I got into the work I'm now doing, because…
- The one thing I thought I could never do without was…
- When the cop pulled me over, I was…
- The first dollar I earned came from…
- My trip to _____ was uneventful until…
- I wanted to go so badly, I decided to…
- The history books should remember me because I…
- I've always been afraid of…
- I laughed because I wanted…
- The competition was tough, so I…
- At the restaurant, I made the mistake of…
- Whenever I see my neighbor, I think about…
- Flowers were appropriate in this situation, but instead…
- Tears came to my eyes when…
- At the wedding, I never expected…
- If I could live anywhere, it wouldn't be…
- This holiday was special because…
- Back where I used to live, I would…
- It had always been a family tradition, until…
- I thought I knew what would happen, but then…
- If I won the lottery, I would…
- Supposing I could live during any age of history, I would choose…
- I set what I thought was the most important goal in my life, and…
- People say it was a miracle when…

- The proudest moment of my life came after…
- Of all the mistakes I've ever made, this one…
- When I need to relax, I like to…
- Our vacation plans looked perfect until…
- When I went to the doctor, I was shocked when he said…
- At school, I got into trouble for…

Scriptures for Storytellers

Psalms

- Let my concepts and writings be acceptable in your sight, O Lord, my strength and my redeemer. — Psalm 19:14
- While waiting for the Lord, write. Be strong and take heart, and keep writing for the Lord. — Psalm 27:14
- My heart overflows with a captivating theme, for my voice is the pen of a skillful writer. — Psalm 45:1
- Come and listen, all who respect God, and I will tell my stories about what he has done for me. — Psalm 66:16
- God's wondrous deeds are more than we can count, so we can tell stories of his righteousness and deliverance all the time, every day. — Psalm 71:15
- By the power of the Holy Spirit, we are skilled communicators of the righteous work that only God can do. — Psalm 71:16
- God, you taught me through experiences when I was young, so now I have great stories to show how marvelous you are. — Psalm 71:17
- God's word is a lamp that lights my writing journey. — Psalm 119:105
- If God is our helper when we write, the stories we build cannot be in vain. — Psalm 127:1
- When I ponder what to write about, I remember the plights of my past and why I now give you praise. Then I reveal your glory by showing how you've worked in my life. — Psalm 143:5

Proverbs

- The words of deceivers shed innocent blood, but godly writing saves lives. — Proverbs 12:6
- Writers rejoice when they can reach their audience with the right words at the right time. — Proverbs 15:23
- Writing sprinkled with humor is wonderful medicine, for pleasant words are like honeycomb, sweet to the soul and healing to the bones. — Proverbs 16:24
- Commit your writing to the Lord, and your message will touch people's hearts. — Proverbs 16:3
- Writers would like to chart their entire journey to success, but God wants them to take the next right step. — Proverbs 16:9
- Writers who develop excellent skills in their work will be admired by their peers and will earn the respect of those they don't know. — Proverbs 22:29
- Without guidance, writers will fail, so blessed are those who carefully follow publishing guidelines. — Proverbs 30:18

Ecclesiastes

- Sow your seeds in the morning and keep writing until dark, for then you may reap a great harvest. — Ecclesiastes 11:6

Isaiah

- Write your message in an article or a book so it may be an everlasting witness. — Isaiah 30:8
- Writers who trust the Lord will find strength in him. They'll be like eagles with spread wings, soaring on the wind. They'll be like the runner who has the stamina to finish the race or the hiker who won't faint when the climbing gets tough. — Isaiah 40:31
- When the Lord's message flows through my pen, it cannot be void of meaning but will always produce results, fulfilling his purpose. It cannot fail. — Isaiah 55:11

Jeremiah

- In devouring your Word, my joy and delight comes from spreading your message, O God of Heaven's writers. — Jeremiah 15:16
- Beyond fantasies and wishful thinking, let writers publish stories that let readers experience truth. — Jeremiah 23:28
- The Lord says, "I know the great things I have in mind for your writing—plans for you to succeed, not fail—so anticipate the future with eager expectation." — Jeremiah 29:11

Ezekiel

- Publish the pieces you have written, so people can read them. — Ezekiel 37:20

Joel

- Write for your children so they can tell their children, so your stories may live from generation to generation. — Joel 1:3

Nahum

- The Lord is good, a wonderful retreat when we suffer from writer's block. He recognizes those who seek him for guidance. — Nahum 1:7

Habakkuk

- Use plainly spoken words so people can easily read my message and run to tell others. — Habakkuk 2:2

Job

- Oh that my words were written with an iron pen on a granite tablet so my story could be read forever. — Job 19:23–24

- I write honestly from my heart, seeking to make the truth known. — Job 33:3

Matthew

When Jesus saw a large audience gathering, he went up on the hillside, and aspiring writers came to him. And he taught them, saying,

- "Blessed are poor and weak writers, for they will seek help and the Kingdom of Heaven belongs to them. — Matthew 5:3
- "Blessed are writers who mourn, who grieve over their lack of success, for God will bring comfort, joy, and laughter to their aching hearts. — Matthew 5:4
- "Blessed are humble writers, those who are content with who they are, for they will discover their unique voice that resonates with their audience. — Matthew 5:5
- "Blessed are those who strive to write their best, who hunger and thirst to please God, for they will find true satisfaction. — Matthew 5:6
- "Blessed are the merciful writers who really care for their audience, for they shall be well cared for. — Matthew 5:7
- "Blessed are writers who are open and honest, concerned about pure motives rather than how they look, for they will walk with God. — Matthew 5:8
- "Blessed are writers who promote peace, who respond to controversy with kindness, for they will be called God's young scribes. — Matthew 5:9
- "Blessed are writers who receive many rejections, whose messages were good but didn't fit the publisher's needs, for the Kingdom of Heaven belongs to them. — Matthew 5:10
- "Blessed are shunned writers, those who are rejected, insulted, and falsely accused because of their Christian perspective. In their day of abuse, they will rejoice because their reward in Heaven is great. The ancient prophetic writers were treated the same way." — Matthew 5:11–12

- "Writers are like the salt that makes food taste good," Jesus said. "But if the salt doesn't make the audience like the taste of the message, where is its value? You have a worst-selling book that will gather dust on the shelf or be thrown away. — Matthew 5:13

- "Like city lights on a hill that cannot be hidden, your testimony should give light to the whole world. — Matthew 5:14

- "Writers do not hide their stories where they cannot be read. They are published in emails, blogs, and books to give light to everyone. — Matthew 5:15

- "Let your writing shine so people may read your words and glorify God in Heaven." — Matthew 5:16

- Writers in the Kingdom of Heaven bring forth treasured stories that are familiar yet refreshingly new. — Matthew 13:52

- Those who have sacrificed possessions, relationships, and pleasures so they can write stories about Christ working in their lives will receive a much greater benefit, as well as eternal life. — Matthew 19:29

John

- For God so loved the world that he gave his only son, so writers who believe in him and share their stories will not die but will lead others to eternal life. — John 3:16

- Like a mighty river, words will flow from the mouth of those who believe in Christ. — John 7:38

Acts

- For you will tell your story to everyone—all you have seen and heard. — Acts 22:15

Romans

- You can be sure your present pain is nothing compared to the value of a finished manuscript when it is published. — Romans 8:18
- Rejections, unreturned calls, and ignored book proposals will all work for good for writers who love God and seek to communicate a message that pleases him. — Romans 8:28
- So what can you say about your writing efforts? If God is on your side, you cannot fail. — Romans 8:31
- Don't let the world around you dictate how you write, but let God change the way you think. Then your stories will be what he wants—good, well-pleasing, and complete. — Romans 12:2

1 Corinthians

- God has chosen our meager writing skills to impact readers more than bestselling authors. He has chosen our small, insignificant words to change lives that were thought to be unchangeable. — 1 Corinthians 1:27
- Because we receive our inspiration from God, not the world, we are able to write about how he has blessed us. — 1 Corinthians 2:12
- Athletes give their lives in strenuous training for a short-lived glory, but writers strive for a reward that will last forever. — 1 Corinthians 9:25
- If I write with human excellence and angelic might without truly caring about my audience, my message is little more than a noisy gong or clanging cymbal. — 1 Corinthians 13:1
- If I write with the skill of a bestselling author, but I do it without love, my book boasts of greatness without any real merit. — 1 Corinthians 13:1

2 Corinthians

- You are expressly purposed through our ministry to be Jesus' letter to the world—not written with pen and ink but by the Spirit of our living God. His message will not be read from stone tablets but from your changed hearts. — 2 Corinthians 3:3

- As we focus on the Lord's presence and write for his glory, all who give themselves to the craft are changed into his image, rising from one publishing success to the next as the Holy Spirit keeps working in our lives. — 2 Corinthians 3:18

Galatians

- Please understand, if you listen to God's Spirit within, you will write to please him and to benefit others, not to satisfy your selfish desires. — Galatians 5:16

Philippians

- Fellow writers, I've not yet become the best I can be, but I know one thing: I need to put past failures and successes behind me and focus on doing much better in the future. — Philippians 3:13

- I place the highest value on the heavenly reward for using my God-given storytelling talent to the best of my ability. — Philippians 3:14

- I can write anything if Christ will give me the ability and stamina. — Philippians 4:13

Colossians

- Whatever you write for people, make your message most pleasing to the Lord, for the greatest reward comes from publishing with him. — Colossians 3:23–24

- Be gracious with your stories, flavoring your message with that which will answer the hunger for God in everyone's heart. — Colossians 4:6

1 Thessalonians

- Pray for the publishing of God's message, so it will be honored among others as it has been in you. — 1 Thessalonians 3:1
- My friends, I beg you to recognize the leaders who work among you to spread the Christian message. Give them your highest love and support for the work they are doing, and live in peace for having done your part. — 1 Thessalonians 5:12-13
- In every acceptance and rejection, give thanks in your writing efforts, because this is God's will for you in Christ Jesus. — 1 Thessalonians 5:18

1 Timothy

- Don't let people despise you as a novice, but be a faith example by seeking excellence in your writing. — 1 Timothy 4:12

James

- What good is it, fellow believers, if you think you should write but fail to do the work? Can your belief alone get your book written? — James 2:14

1 Peter

- Make good on your commitment to the Lord by preparing to share your experiences with those who might not understand how you have survived your struggles. Always be ready to reveal why you have hope in this tumultuous world. — 1 Peter 3:15
- My dear storytellers, don't be unduly alarmed by the fiery ordeals that come to test your writing ability, as if this were an abnormal experience. — 1 Peter 4:12

- Respecting God's ability above your own, humble yourselves, and God will cause your writing effort to prosper in due time. — 1 Peter 5:6
- Yes, for as long as I can tell the story, I have a responsibility to refresh your memory of what Jesus means to you. — 2 Peter 1:13

Recommended Resources

God, you taught me through experiences when I
was young, so now I have great stories to show
how marvelous you are. — Psalm 71:17

In our age of technology, you can learn online all the information and misinformation that a person could ever want. If only you knew where to look and what to search for.

Here are a few resources that writers have found helpful:

- *Book Proposal Tips and Tricks* by Steve Laube
- OneLook.com — a free online dictionary research tool
- *Proofreading Secrets of Best-Selling Authors* by Kathy Ide
- *Story Trumps Structure* by Steven James
- *The Christian Writers Market Guide* online subscription (ChristianWritersMarketGuide.com), always up-to-date, only $9.99 per year
- *The Christian Publishing Show* podcasts with Thomas Umstattd Jr (ChristianWritersInstitute.com/podcasts/)
- Udemy.com — huge library of economical training videos
- *Write with Excellence 201* by Joyce Ellis
- *Writer to Writer: Lessons from a Lifetime of Writing* by Cecil Murphey
- *Writing the Breakout Novel* by Donald Maass

About the Author

*My heart overflows with a captivating theme, for my
voice is the pen of a skillful writer. Psalm 45:1*

After thirty years of computer programming and business
administration, Frank abandoned the technology he loved most
to pursue what he hated most: writing and teaching. Why? Several
vivid dreams led him to believe God wanted his life to go in a
different direction. Therefore, in the last thirty years, writing and
teaching have been among his greatest treasures in life.

He learned that if people want to experience God and fulfill
The Great Commission, they need to tell their life-changing
stories. Well-crafted stories deliver an experience of truth that the
audience can't reject.

For ten years, he directed North Texas Christian Writers to
help members improve their writing and storytelling skills. In
2018, he joined the Roaring Lambs ministry to encourage and
equip all Christians to tell their life-changing stories. He has
taught at writing conferences and churches across the U.S. and
Canada. Besides writing his own books, he does ghostwriting,
editing, and graphic design to
help others publish high-
quality books.

A widower since 2003, he
has three married sons, seven
grandchildren and lives in a
Fort Worth, Texas, suburb.

Made in the USA
Coppell, TX
07 June 2024

33187070R00138